AIR FRYER

Cookbook for Beginners

550 Easy-to-Remember Delicious Air Fryer Recipes for Smart and Busy People

By

Alexandra Bryne

Disclaimer

Please note, the information written in this book, are for educational and entertainment purposes only. Strenuous efforts have been made to provide accurate, up to date and reliable complete information in this book. All recommendations are made without guarantee on the part of the author and publisher. By reading this document, the reader agrees that under no circumstances are we responsible for any losses, direct or indirect, which are incurred as a result of the use of the information contained in this document, including but not limited to errors, omissions or inaccuracies.

Table of Contents

KW-223-049

Introduction
Welcome to Air fryer cookbook

New to Air Fryer? Congratulations and welcome aboard to the world of fast and easy cooking. The Air Fryer is a kitchenware that makes use of Rapid Air Technology or hot air to cook the kind of meals that would traditionally be dunked in a deep fat fryer. It has a mechanical fan that circulates the hot air around the food at high speed, cooking the food and producing a crispy layer via the Maillard effect.

Traditional frying methods induce the Maillard effect by completely submerging foods in hot oil. The air fryer works alternatively by coating the desired food in a thin layer of oil while circulating air heated up to 200°C to confer energy and initiate the reaction. They cook with very hot circulating air and provide a healthier alternative to conventional frying because they use little or no oil.

While Air Fryers technically cook by convection roasting rather than frying, it can still deliver results similar to the real frying. Convection ovens and air fryers are very similar in terms of how they cook food, but air fryers are generally smaller than convection ovens and give off less heat when cooking. Similar results can be achieved by using specialized air crisper trays and putting them in the oven. Air fryers are attractive for their convenience, safety, and health benefits.

This **Air fryer cookbook for Beginners** consists of 11 chapters specifically written for fried favourites. The recipes are quick and delicious for healthy living. You can bake, grill, roast, and fry any of the recipes with your Air Fryer. Delicious recipes written in this cookbook varies from breakfast, lunch and vegan, side dishes, appetizers, fish and seafoods, meat, pork and beef, poultry, desserts, and ketogenic diets. Foods taste much the same as they do if they are conventionally deep fried – you get the crunch, the browning and the tantalizing aroma as well. With your Air Fryer, you can actually be able to eat a healthier version of fried foods.

The Basics of Air Frying

Air fryers are modern machines that use innovative air circulation and heat transfer technology to fry and cook foods without oil or grease. Air fryers are modern, revolutionized kitchen appliances that make use of superheated air to cook and fry foods. They are able to produce that crunch on the outside and softness inside which is usually associated with deep-frying so the foods are very similar in taste to actual fat-fried foods.

It is a compact cylindrical countertop convection oven. An Air Fryer is a kitchen appliance that makes use of superheated air to cook foods that is related to deep-frying or high-temperature roasting. It is a kitchen appliance that allows you multiple cooking choices such as frying, baking, roasting and grilling. Majority of us may have convection ovens in our kitchens. But in a standard oven, the air is heated and that hot air in a high temperature cooks the food.

Air fryers have revolutionized conventional deep frying into a quick, healthy and safe process. Air fryers are modern, revolutionized kitchen devices that make use of superheated air to cook and fry foods. You can now look forward to cooking favorite fried foods for your family without the accompanying feelings of guilt. In a convection oven, the air that is heated is usually blown around by a fan. This procedure of creating hot air produces more energy and subsequently cooks the foods faster. The same mechanism of convention ovens is also used by Air Fryers. But the foods in Air Fryers is cooked by the hot air blown around in a compact cylinder and the food sits in a perforated basket.

The Air Fryer is more efficient than the convention ovens because it creates an intense environment of heat from which the food cannot escape. Air-fried foods has a crispy brown exterior and moist tender interior without all the oil and fat needed to deep-fry. The little oil makes a refreshing contrast with the enormous puddles of oil that you'd need to use for deep frying foods. Air frying helps reduce fat-laden calories and thereby decreases innate health risks including obesity etc.

Health Benefits of Air Frying Your Foods

Air Fryers produce results similar to deep-frying using a little quantity of the oil needed to deep-fry. When deep-frying, you completely submerge the food in oil and the oil is absorbed by the food. In an Air Fryer, you will make use of a tiny fraction of oil to help crisp and brown the foods. The health benefits of air frying include:

1. Fast and Energy Efficient:

The Air Fryer can prepare delicious foods quickly and efficiently. While it can take a while for the oven to heat up, your air fryer will heat up within minutes. Most air-fried meals can be prepared in just minutes! While it takes about 15 to 20 minutes to pre-heat our standard ovens, it takes the Air Fryer about 2 to 3 minutes because the Air Fryer is pretty much compacted. That's a huge savings in time as well as energy. During the summer, your Air Fryer can be pre-heated without heating up your whole kitchen.

The intense heat generated in the Air Fryer cooks foods quickly, about 20% faster than in an oven. It simply means that Air Fryers save more time and energy.

2. No Pollution:

Most stoves and gas cookers automatically result in some form of environmental pollution or hazards. Air fryers come equipped with cooling systems that keep the machine free from contamination. The Air Fryer has some mechanism for cooling and filtering the heated air before being released into the air. The air filter also prevents the soggy smell of oil from spreading around the kitchen. You can expect to enjoy fresh kitchen smells before and after cooking with an air fryer!

3. Easy to Use:

The Air Fryer is incredibly easy to use. Air-frying is safer and easier than deep-frying. Majority of Air Fryers have different settings for time and temperature. There is need to simply enter both and press start. When deep-frying, it involves heating a large pot of oil on the stovetop and makes use of a deep-frying thermometer to measure the temperature and monitor the heat below the pot to maintain that temperature. It is simply difficult and unsafe because you are dealing with a lot of oil, which can be heavy to move, and very dangerous to handle if it gets too hot.

4. Clean and Tidy:

We know you would love keeping your kitchen clean and tidy when cooking and after cooking. Deep fryers often result in a messy kitchen. Because an air fryer uses no oil, there aren't any messy clean-ups. The food cooks inside an enclosed fryer, so there's no risk of spills or splatters anywhere. Clean-up after meal is simple and straightforward, which is especially important for time-crunched moms. The entire system is non-stick, and the fryer basket is dishwasher-safe, which makes clean-up quick, simple and painless.

5. Safe to use:

Most models of Air Fryers come equipped with an automatic shutdown feature that switches off the machine when the food is cooked. The air fryer has a variety of safety features that make it safe for even newbies to use. With the auto-shutoff feature, you don't have to worry about forgetting to turn the fryer off. Secondly, there's no oil or open flame, which minimizes the risk of kitchen fires and other mishaps. There's no risk of injury due to oil splatters.

Working Mechanism of Your Air Fryer

The Air Fryer works by making use of the rapid air technology system which is a combination of high velocity hot air circulation and grilling. The rapid air technology ensures that the hot air circulates with high speed around all the content in the Air Fryer basket. Air fryers makes use of what is called the 'Rapid Air Technology' to cook different types of foods that we'd otherwise fry by dipping them in hot fat. This Rapid Air technology works by heating air up to high temperatures (200°C or 400°F) and frying foods like pastries, chicken, fish and chips.

Air Fryers use a combination of high temperature and high speed of air circulation along with a top grill in order to help fry foods. In other words, air fryers use air instead of oil to carry heat and cook foods; air plays a crucial role. This simply implies that the cooking basket gets the heat from all sides evenly, and the food is being cooked at a faster rate.

The rapid air technology enables the food to become crunchier on the outside, while being tender and moist on the inside. The Air Fryers rapid air technology is comprised of two systems. The first system comprises of the exhaust system that controls the temperature of the fryer, alongside with the internal pressure. This exhaust system resolves the issues of excessive air. It also comprises of a filter which filters the excessive air in the system before the final release.

As a result of that, the foods cooked in an Air Fryer retains no odor of cooking or smoke spreads throughout your kitchen. The second part of the system was designed to control the internal temperature of the Air Fryer. It consists of a cooling fan that ensures the circulation of fresh air goes from top to bottom. As a result of the second part of the system, the internal parts of the Air Fryer remain cool, while at the same time, the air used in cooking remains scorching hot. This cooling system enables you to cook in hot weather, for example during the summer season, while your kitchen does not become any hotter because of this kitchen appliance.

Smart Tips and Tricks for Using Your Air fryer

- You have to preheat your Air Fryer for an average of 3 minutes to get the desired temperature. After placing the ingredients in the basket or cooking pot, you have to ensure that there is enough space for the hot air to pass around.

- When you want to prepare pre-made food, like French fries, set the temperature of your Air Fryer to Lower by 70°C than what's standard, and reduce the cooking time on the timer by half for about 15-20 minutes. Although, the temperature and time measurement sure can vary, depending on the type and size of food you're cooking.

- Make use of a non-stick pan or cooking basket to cook and add a drop of oil on the bottom of the pot. When you want to prepare food with excessive fat, for example chicken drumsticks, you should remove any splattering and/or excess vapor and drain the fat.

- Always shake the basket at about half of the cooking dish to ensure that the meal is evenly browned and cooked through. After cooking fatty foods, clean the fat on the bottom of the ingredients after you've finished cooking your meal.

- You should find time to clean your Air Fryer with hot water and low to medium-hard sponge after every single use of the Air Fryer. Dry the Air Fryer with a paper towel after clean with hot water.

General Tips for Air Frying Your Foods

1. Preparing to Air-fry:

Keep the Air Fryer in a suitable position in your kitchen. Place your Air Fryer on a level, heat-resistant countertop and ensure that there are at least 5-inches of space behind the Air Fryer where the exhaust vent is located.

Preheat the Air Fryer before adding your food into the Air Fryer basket. Turn your Air Fryer to the exact temperature that you need and set the timer for about 2 or 3 minutes. When the timer goes off, the Air Fryer has preheated and ready to place your food.

Buy lots of kitchen spray bottles to spraying oil on the food and it is better than drizzling or brushing which allows you to use less oil.

2. Get the Right Accessories:

When you start air frying, there is need to invest in some accessories for your new kitchen appliance. Baking dishes or cake pans that are oven-safe are also air fryer-safe as well since they do not come in contact with the heating element. The accessory pan needs to fit inside the air fryer basket.

Make an aluminum foil sling to place the accessory pieces into and out of the air fryer basket. The piece of aluminum foil sling has to be folded into a strip about 2-inches wide by 24-inches long. Carefully place the cake pan or baking dish on the foil and by holding the ends of the foil, it will enable you to lift the pan or dish and lower it into the air fryer basket.

Fold the ends of the piece of aluminum foil into the Air Fryer basket, and then return the basket to your Air Fryer. Once you have finished cooking, carefully remove the pan, unfold and hold onto the ends of the aluminum foil to lift the pan out from the basket of your Air Fryer.

3. While You Are Air-Frying:

Add enough water when you are cooking fatty foods. Adding enough water to the drawer underneath the basket when cooking helps to prevent grease from getting too hot and smoking. This should be done especially when cooking bacon, sausage, and burgers.

Make use of toothpicks to hold your foods down. This is because the fan from the Air Fryer usually pick up light foods and blow them around when cooking. Therefore, it is advisable to secure foods like the top slice of bread on a sandwich with toothpicks.

Avoid overcrowding the basket. You may prefer to cook your food at one time, but over-crowding the basket will prevent the foods from crisping and browning evenly. So, it's important to cook some of your foods in batches to avoid over-crowding the basket.

Flip the foods over halfway through the cooking time so that they can brown evenly.

4. Shake the Basket While Cooking:

Shake the basket severally during the cooking process to re-distribute the ingredients and enable them to crisp and brown evenly. If there is more than one layer of ingredients in the basket or many ingredients touch each other such as fries and snacks shaking halfway through the process is necessary for an even result. Fragile food should not be air fried in more than one layer, as shaking will damage it the tender foods.

If you do not shake, the hot air cannot reach the areas where the ingredients touch each other. The food in the basket will be cooked, but some areas will not get crispy. By shaking, your food will become more evenly colored and crispier all over. When you shake the basket, you can also check on the color of the ingredients. Spray the basket with spraying oil to get the food to brown and crisp more. Also, spritz it with olive oil during the cooking process to enable the food to brown more evenly.

5. After You Air-Fry:

It is important to remove the Air Fryer basket from the drawer before turning out foods. Do not invert the basket while the basket is still locked into the Air Fryer drawer, it will lead to dumping of all the rendered fat or excess grease onto your plate along with the food you just air-fried.

Don't empty the juices from the drawer too soon because the drawer collects a lot of juices from the cooked foods and catches any marinades that you pour over the food. The flavorful liquid can be served as a sauce to pour over food if the drippings are not too greasy.

6. Clean the Drawer and The Basket After Every Use:

The drawer of your Air Fryer is very easy to clean and when you leave it unwashed, it will lead to the risk of food contamination and your kitchen won't have a nice smell. So, it's very important to wash and clean the drawer and the basket after preparing your meals.

7. Use the Air Fryer to Dry Itself:

Once you have finished washing the Air Fryer basket and drawer, just pop them back into your Air Fryer and turn it on for about 2 to 3 minutes. Both parts will dry itself better than any drying towel.

8. Re-heating Your Foods in The Air Fryer:

There's no exact time and temperature when re-heating leftovers because leftovers vary so significantly. We recommend re-heating your foods in the Air Fryer at 350°F.

Trouble-shooting Tips

Air fryers are solid little machines, but as with any appliance, things can go wrong. Much of what goes wrong with an air fryer can be traced to human error. Here are some problems that are usually due to user confusion and how to correct them:

1. **Lingering food odors:**

The air fryer needs to be cleaned regularly immediately after each meal to avoid lingering odors. Convection cooking sprays tiny particles of food around more than conventional cooking does.

2. **When your food does not turn out as crispy as expected:**

It is pretty much possible to cook crispy potatoes, snacks, meat, poultry or breaded snacks in your Air Fryer. But other foods, such as vegetables, will never get crispy when prepared in the Air Fryer. If you want to obtain crispy results with food that can be air fried, you have to ensure that you are not over-crowding the Air Fryer basket and make use of a tiny fraction of oil. Always shake the basket severally while cooking to ensure even browning and crispiness.

3. **Difficulty of sliding the outer basket into place:**

This is similar to other smaller kitchen appliances such as food processors, juicers, and mixers, all of the parts of an Air Fryers have to be inserted correctly or the appliance won't fit together. Once the basket won't slide in, reassemble the other parts and ensure that they fit snugly and try again. Carefully lift the basket a little while sliding it to position it correctly again.

4. **The Air Fryer is hot to the touch:**

As with any cooking appliance excepting microwaves, Air Fryers become hot to be touched while in use. Always ensure that your Air Fryer is out of reach to your children while cooking to avoid hurting them.

5. **When there is a white smoke coming from the Air Fryer:**

Whenever there is a white smoke coming out from your Air Fryer, add a little amount of water to the Air Fryer drawer underneath the basket. The white smoke is usually as a result of grease that has drained into the drawer and is burning. Adding some water to the drawer will prevent the smoke from coming out.

6. **When there is a black smoke coming from the Air Fryer:**

Kindly turn off the Air Fryer machine and look up towards the heating element inside the fryer. It may be caused as a result of some foods that might have blown up and attached to the heating element, burning and causing the black smoke.

7. **When the Air Fryer machine won't turn off:**

Some of the modern Air Fryers are designed to have a delay in their shutting down process. Immediately you press the power button off, the fan inside the Air Fryer will continue to blow the hot air out of the unit for about 20 seconds. Desist yourself from pressing button again to avoid complications. Exercise some patient and wait for the Air Fryer to turn off.

Air Fryer Recipes Conversion

1. Converting from Traditional Recipes:

The Air Fryer can be used to cook recipes that have instructions for cooking in the oven. This is as a result of the fact that heat in the air fryer is more intense than a standard oven, reduce the suggested temperature by 25°F – 50°F and reduce the time by roughly 20%. So, a recipe that is meant to be cooked at 400°F for 20 minutes, Air-fry at 370°F for about 16 minutes.

2. Converting from Packaged Foods Instructions:

The same uniform rule applies to prepared foods that you may purchase in a grocery store. If a bag of frozen French fries recommends cooking in the conventional oven at 450°F for about 18 minutes, you can cook that same French fries in your Air Fryer at 400°F and start checking them at about 15 minutes. Always remember to shake the basket once or twice during the cooking process to enable the French fries to crisp and brown evenly.

3. Converting to Different Sized Air-Fryers:

Larger Air Fryers can make it easier, especially when you are cooking for 4 or more people because the Air Fryer baskets in these Air Fryers are larger in size. The larger sized Air Fryers will enable you to cook more food at one time and do not have to cook the food in batches.

Always remember not to over-crowd the Air Fryer basket because it will slow down the overall cooking time and result in foods that are not as crispy and evenly browned. Some larger Air Fryers possesses more power to cook foods slightly faster than smaller, lower wattage Air Fryers.

Air Fryers Buyer's Guide

Most Air Fryers look similar, but they don't have the same functionality or features. Here are some of the things you should be aware of when buying your Air Fryer.

1. **Timer:**

The timer varies but can either be a digital or analog implementation. Since food items cook quickly in air fryers, majority of Air Fryers have timers that can be set up to about 30 minutes. If you budget to cook your food for longer, it would be wise to buy an Air Fryer that can go up to 60 minutes.

The analog dials are easier to use, but they usually have some drawbacks because some timers will keep on ticking when the drawer housing the food is removed. Air Fryer with a digital timer tends to be better and more accurate with time keeping but they also tend to be costlier.

2. **Temperature Setting:**

Different foods require different temperatures to achieve optimal results. Some foods such as pork or bacon will require different temperature settings than cooking potato wedges. Majority of Air Fryers comes with a range of roughly 200°F – 400°F which is plenty of variation to cook a wide variety of food items.

It's worthy of note that if your Air Fryer can't reach a certain temperature that is required for a particular recipe, all you have to do is to cook the food longer. The temperature settings can be implemented either digitally or via an analog display too.

3. **Size and Capacity:**

Air Fryers comprises of a variety of sizes and the capacity is measured in quarts, pounds, or liters. You should buy a smaller unit if you aim to be cooking for one or two people or you are cooking smaller units of food. Larger Air Fryers should be considered for purchase if you want to cook larger quantities of food for more people two people.

4. **Pre-set Cooking Programs:**

The pre-set cooking programs of digital Air Fryers enables you to automatically set the time and temperature by the pushing of a button for a number of common food items. Some Air Fryers have their functional settings printed on their lid or body.

5. **Safety features:**

Most Air Fryers today come with a host of safety features. These safety features include a cool touch handle, a safety button on the handle to prevent the Air Fryer basket from falling when taking out your food, and an automatic shut off ability when the timer expires. Air Fryers are designed to prevent the smoke from building up and also protect the internal components from getting dirty or damaged.

6. **Cleaning:**

The components of the Air Fryers that usually gets dirty such as the bottom drawer and basket are dishwasher safe. This implies that you can throw them in the dishwasher for a good clean. The majority of parts of this home device are removable as well as dishwasher-safe. This which means that you no longer need to use up too much of your time to scrape the pan as well as strive to make sure every little thing is tidy. Some components like a mesh basket or grated grill are prone to food items becoming stuck on them and so it is necessary to clean them in dishwater.

7. **Accessories**

Some accessories like mesh basket, racks and tongs comes along with a newly purchased Air Fryer. These accessories make it easier to have grill racks and pans to help handle other food items more comfortably.

Measurement & Conversions

Metric to Standard	Fahrenheit to Celsius Scale	Pounds to Kilograms	Cups to Tablespoons	Ounce to Grams
5 ml = 1 tsp	250°F = 120°C	1 lb. = 0.45 kg	3 tsp = 1 tbsp	1 oz = 29 g
15 ml = 1 tbsp	300°F = 150°C	2 lb. = 0.91 kg	1/8 cup = 2 tbsp	2 oz = 57 g
30 ml = 1 fluid oz	350°F = 180°C	3 lb. = 1.36 kg	¼ cup = 4 tbsp	3 oz = 85 g
240 ml = 1 cup	375°F = 190°C	4 lb. = 1.81 kg	1/3 cup = 1 tbsp + 1 tsp	4 oz = 113 g
1 liter = 34 fluid oz	400°F =200°C	5 lb. = 2.27 kg	½ cup = 8 tbsp	5 oz = 142 g
1 liter = 4.2 cups	425°F = 220°C	6 lb. = 2.72 kg	¾ cup = 12 tbsp	6 oz = 170 g
1 gram = .035 oz	450°F = 230°C	7 lb. = 3.18 kg	1 cup = 16 tbsp	7 oz = 198 g
100 grams = 3.5 oz	475°F = 250°C	8 lb. = 3.63 kg	8 fluid oz = 1 cup	8 oz = 227 g
		9 lb. = 4.06 kg		9 oz = 255 g
				10 oz = 283 g
				11 oz = 311 g

Abbreviations

- tsp. = teaspoon
- tbsp. = tablespoon
- lb. = pound
- lbs.= pounds
- c = cup
- oz = ounce
- ml = milliliter
- kg = kilogram
- g = gram
- fl. oz = fluid ounce
- pt. = pint
- qt = quart
- gal = gallon
- L = liter

CHAPTER 1: DELICIUOS BREAKFAST RECIPES

Home Fried Potatoes

Preparation time: 30 minutes

Cooking time: 35 minutes

Overall time: 1 hour 5 minutes

Serves: 3 to 4 people

Recipe Ingredients:

- 3 large potatoes (scrubbed and diced into ½ - ¾ cubes)
- 1 medium onion diced
- 1 small red pepper diced (optional)
- 2 tbsp. of bacon grease Or Olive oil Or Coconut oil
- 2 tsp. of sea salt or smoked salt
- 1 tsp. of onion powder
- 1 tsp. of garlic powder
- 1 tsp. paprika

Cooking Directions:

1. In a large bowl, Place the scrubbed/diced potatoes. Cover with water and soak for about 20 to 30 minutes.

2. Then mix all seasonings together and reserve aside, grease the bottom of the Air Fryer Basket with coconut oil.

3. After soaking the potatoes, drain the potatoes, dry well and place into large mixing bowl.

4. Add the Bacon Grease to the potatoes and mix thoroughly. After mixing the potatoes with oil.

5. Place the Oiled potatoes into your Air Fryer Basket and set the Basket into your Air Fryer.

6. Keep the mixing bowl for the onions and peppers aside. Set your Air Fryer to cook the potatoes at 370 degrees for about 20 minutes.

7. Shake several times during cooking cycle. Dice the onions and red peppers, place it into a mixing bowl and set aside until Air Fryer is done cooking.

8. When the time is up, transfer the potatoes into the bowl with onions and peppers and mix through.

9. Add the seasonings and mix through. Add the mixture into your Air Fryer Basket and place into the Air Fryer.

10. Set your Air Fryer to cook at 380 degrees for about 5 to 10 minutes more.

11. Shake several times during cooking cycle or until potatoes are browned and onions are soft.

Breakfast Frittata

Recipe Ingredients:

- 3 eggs
- ½ Italian sausage
- 4 cherry tomatoes (in half)
- 1 tbsp. of olive oil
- Chopped parsley
- Grano Padano cheese Or parmesan
- Salt and pepper

Cooking Instructions:

1. Preheat your Air Fryer to about 360 degrees. Then place the cherry tomatoes and sausage in the baking accessory.

2. Bake at 360 degrees for about 5 minutes. Whisk the remaining ingredients together in a small mixing bowl.

3. Now remove the baking accessory from your Air Fryer, add the egg mixture, making sure it is even.

4. Bake for another 5 minutes. After baking for 5 minutes.

5. Serve and enjoy!

Parmesan Cauliflower Steak

Serves: 3 to 4 people

Recipe Ingredients:

- 1 large head cauliflower
- 4 tablespoons of butter
- 2 tbsp. of urban accents Manchego and roasted garlic seasoning blend
- ¼ cup of parmesan cheese
- Salt and pepper

Cooking Instructions:

1. Preheat your oven to about 400 degrees. Remove leaves from cauliflower.

2. Slice cauliflower lengthwise through core into 1-inch steaks. Then melt butter in your microwave, mix butter with seasoning blend to make paste.

3. Brush the paste mixture over steaks, season with salt and pepper to taste. Heat non-stick pan over medium.

4. Place cauliflower steaks for 2 to 3 minutes until lightly browned, flip carefully, repeat.

5. Then place cauliflower steaks on lined baking sheet and bake cauliflower steaks in oven for 15-20 minutes. (until golden and tender).

6. After baking for 15 to 20 minutes, sprinkle with parmesan cheese.

7. Serve immediately and enjoy!

French Toast Sticks

Preparation time: 6 minutes

Cooking time: 12 minutes

Total time: 18 minutes

Recipe Ingredients:

- 4 pieces of sliced bread
- 2 tablespoons approximately of soft butter or margarine for buttering bread
- 2 eggs gently beaten
- Salt
- Cinnamon
- Nutmeg
- Ground cloves
- Icing sugar OR maple syrup for garnish

Cooking Instructions:

1. First preheat your Air fryer to 180° Celsius.

2. In a medium mixing bowl, beat two eggs together and sprinkle of salt, a few heavy shakes of cinnamon, small pinches of both nutmeg and ground cloves.

3. Butter both sides of the bread slices, cut the bread into strips, Dredge each strip in the egg mixture.

4. Place and arrange and arrange it in your Air fryer (cook in two batches) after 2 minutes of cooking.

5. Pause the Air fryer, take out the pan, ensure that the pan is kept on a heat safe surface.

6. Spray the bread with cooking spray. Once you have coated the strips thoroughly, flip and spray the second side as well.

7. Then return the pan to your Air fryer and cook for more 4 minutes. Keep checking it after a couple of minutes to make sure they are cooking evenly.

8. When the egg is cooked and bread is golden brown. Sprinkle with icing sugar, top with whip cream, drizzle with maple syrup if you desire.

9. Serve immediately and enjoy!

Tofu Scramble

Preparation time: 5 minutes

Cooking time: 30 minutes

Total time: 35 minutes

Serves: 3 to 4 people

Recipe Ingredients:

- 1 block tofu (chopped into 1" pieces)
- 2 tbsp. of soy sauce
- 1 tbsp. of olive oil
- 1 tsp. of turmeric
- ½ tsp. of garlic powder
- ½ tsp. of onion powder
- ½ cup of chopped onion
- 2½ cups of chopped red potato - 1" cubes, 2 to 3 potatoes
- 1 tbsp. of olive oil
- 4 cups of broccoli florets

Cooking Instructions:

1. In a mixing bowl, toss together the tofu, soy sauce, olive oil, turmeric, garlic powder, onion powder, and onion.

2. Set aside to marinate. Then toss the potatoes and the olive oil in a separate small bowl.

3. Air fry at 400°F for about 15 minutes. shake once around 7 to 8 minutes into cooking. Shake the potatoes and add the tofu, reserving any leftover marinade.

4. Set the tofu and potatoes to cook at 370°F for another 15 minutes, and start the air fryer.

5. During the tofu cooking process, toss the broccoli in the reserved marinade. If there isn't enough to get it all over the broccoli.

6. Add a little bit of extra soy sauce. When there are 5 minutes of cooking time remaining, add in the broccoli to the Air fryer.

7. When the time is up, serve and enjoy!

Blueberry Lemon Muffin

Preparation time: 7 minutes

Cooking time: 10 to 12 minutes

Total time: 15 to 25 minutes

Yield: 1 dz.

Recipe Ingredients:

- 2½ cups of self-rising flour
- ½ cup of monk fruit
- ½ cup of cream
- ¼ cup of avocado oil (any light cooking oil)
- 2 eggs
- 1 cup of blueberries
- Zest from 1 lemon
- Juice from 1 lemon
- 1 teaspoon of vanilla
- Brown sugar for topping

Cooking Instructions:

1. Mix the self-rising flour and sugar together in a mixing bowl. Reserve aside.

2. Combine the cream, oil, lemon juice, eggs and vanilla together in a medium bowl.

3. Add the flour mixture to the liquid mixture and give everything a good stir until blended. Then stir in the blueberries.

4. Spoon the batter into silicone cupcake holders and sprinkle ½ teaspoon of brown sugar on top of each muffin.

5. Bake at 320° for about 10 minutes, check muffins at 6 minutes to make sure that they are not cooking too fast.

6. Place a toothpick into the center of the muffin. When the toothpick comes out clean and the muffins have browned, they are done.

7. Remove and cool. Serve and enjoy!

Monte Cristo Sandwich

Serves: 1

Recipe Ingredients:

- 1 egg
- 3 tbsp. half and half
- ¼ tsp. of vanilla extract
- 2 slices sourdough, white or multigrain bread
- 2½ oz. of sliced Swiss cheese
- 2 oz. slices deli ham
- 2 oz. of sliced deli turkey
- 1 tsp. of butter, melted
- Powdered sugar
- Raspberry jam, for serving

Cooking Instructions:

1. In a shallow bowl, combine egg, half and half and vanilla extract.

2. Place bread on the counter and build a sandwich with one slice of Swiss cheese, ham, turkey.

3. Place the second slice of Swiss cheese on one slice of the bread. Top with the other slice of bread and press down to flatten.

4. Then preheat your Air fryer to 350°F. Cut out a piece of aluminum foil that is the same size as the bread.

5. Brush the foil with melted butter and dip both sides of the sandwich in the egg batter.

6. Allow the batter to soak into bread for 30 seconds on each side. Place the sandwich on the greased aluminum foil.

7. Transfer it to the Air fryer basket. Brush the top of the sandwich with melted butter for extra browning.

8. After brushing the top of the sandwich, Air-fry at 350°F for 10 about minutes.

9. Flip the sandwich over and brush with butter, Air-fry for an additional 8 minutes.

10. After the 8 minutes, transfer the sandwich to a serving plate and sprinkle with powdered sugar.

11. Serve immediately with raspberry or blackberry preserves on the side.

Donuts Recipe

Recipe Ingredients:

- 1 can Pillsbury Grands Flaky Layers biscuits (8 biscuits; We used Hy-Vee biscuits)
- 3 tbsp. of melted butter
- 1/3 cup of granulated sugar
- ½ to 1 tsp. of cinnamon (adjust to your taste)
- 4 tbsp. of dark brown sugar (break up any clumps)
- Pinch of allspice

Cooking Instructions:

1. In a small mixing bowl, combine the sugar, cinnamon, brown sugar, and allspice. reserve aside.

2. Then remove biscuits from can (do not flatten). Use a 1-inch circle biscuit cutter to cut the holes out of the center of each biscuit.

3. Air-fry the Donuts at 350°F for about 5 minutes (We fried 4 at a time). Air-fry the holes at 350°F for just 3 minutes (We fried all 8 holes at once).

4. As each batch of donuts and holes comes out of your fryer. Use a pastry brush to paint butter over the entire surface of each donut and hole.

5. After painting each donut and hole with butter. Place them into the bowl with the sugar mixture, coat thoroughly with the mixture.

6. Gently shake off excess. Serve donuts and holes immediately and enjoy!

Breakfast Sausage Wraps

Recipe Ingredients:

- 8 Heat N' Serve Sausages
- 2 Pieces of American Cheese (cut into ¼'s)
- 1 can of 8 count refrigerated crescent roll dough
- 8 wooden skewers
- Syrup, ketchup or BBQ for dipping.

Cooking Instructions:

1. First separate crescent rolls on a flat surface. Open sausages and cut cheese.

2. Then place one crescent roll on the surface, unrolled. Work from wide triangle to tip of the triangle.

3. Add the sausage and cheese strip to the Widest part of the crescent roll. Pull each end over sausage and cheese.

4. Roll and tuck the remaining dough until you reach the tip of the triangle. Ensure to pinch all the dough.

5. Place up to 4 of these in your Air fryer and Air-fry at 380° for about 3 minutes (or 4 until golden brown).

6. After the 3 minutes, remove and add in skewer. Tray and serve with BBQ, Ketchup or Syrup for dunking.

7. Serve immediately and enjoy!

Flourless Broccoli Cheese Quiche

Preparation time: 10 minutes

Cooking time: 40 minutes

Total time: 50 mins

Serves: 2-3 people

Recipe Ingredients:

- 1 large broccoli
- 3 large carrots
- 1 large tomato
- 100 g of cheddar cheese grated
- 20 g of feta cheese
- 150 ml whole milk
- 2 large eggs
- 1 tsp. of parsley
- 1 teaspoon of thyme
- Salt & pepper to taste

Cooking Instructions:

1. First chop up the broccoli into florets, peel and dice the carrots.

2. Then add the carrots and broccoli into a food steamer, cook for about 20 minutes or until soft.

3. Add all the seasonings in a measuring jug and crack the eggs into the jug. Then mix everything together.

4. Add the milk gradually until you have a pale mixture. Once the steamer has finished drain the vegetables, line the bottom of your quiche dish with them.

5. Layer with the tomatoes, add your cheese on top. Now pour the liquid over and add a little bit more cheese on top.

6. Place in your Air fryer and cook for about 20 minutes at 180° C.

7. When the time is up, serve and enjoy!

Chocolate Chip Oatmeal Cookies

Total time: 30 minutes

Preparation time: 20 minutes

Bake time: 10 minutes/batch

Makes: about 6 dozen

Recipe Ingredients:

- 1 cup of butter (softened)
- ¾ cup of sugar
- ¾ cup of packed brown sugar
- 2 large eggs
- 1 tsp. of vanilla extract
- 3 cups of quick-cooking oats
- 1½ cups all-purpose flour
- 1 package (3.4 oz.) instant vanilla pudding mix
- 1 tsp. of baking soda
- 1 tsp. of salt
- 2 cups (12 oz.) semisweet chocolate chips
- 1 cup of chopped nuts

Cooking Instructions:

1. First preheat your Air fryer to 350°F and line the air fryer basket with foil.

2. In a large mixing bowl, mix together cream butter and sugars until light and fluffy.

3. Beat in eggs and vanilla. Mix the oats, flour, dry pudding mix, baking soda and salt together to combine well.

4. Gradually add to creamed mixture and mix everything together. Stir in chocolate chips and nuts.

5. Form into balls using one tbsp. of dough, flatten slightly. Place shaped dough 2 in. apart onto foil-lined air fryer basket.

6. Air-fry for about 8 to 10 minutes (until lightly browned). Then remove to wire racks and repeat with the remaining dough.

7. When the time is up, serve and enjoy!

Green Tomato BLT

Total Time

Preparation time: 20 minutes

Cooking time: 10 minutes/batch

Serve: 3 to 4 people

Recipe Ingredients:

- 2 medium green tomatoes (about 10 oz.)
- ½ tsp. of salt
- ¼ tsp. of pepper
- 1 large egg, beaten
- ¼ cup all-purpose flour
- 1 cup panko (Japanese) bread crumbs
- ½ cup of reduced-fat mayonnaise
- 2 green onions (finely chopped)
- 1 tsp. of snipped fresh dill OR ¼ tsp. of dill weed
- 8 slices whole wheat bread, toasted
- 8 cooked center-cut bacon strips
- 4 Bibb or Boston lettuce leaves

Cooking Instructions:

1. First preheat your Air fryer to 350°. Spritz the air fryer basket with cooking spray.

2. Then cut the tomato into eight slices, about ¼ in. thick each. Sprinkle tomato slices with salt and pepper.

3. In a separate bowls, place the egg, flour and bread crumbs. Dip tomato slices in flour, shaking off excess.

4. Dip into egg, and finally dip into bread crumb mixture, patting to help adhere.

5. Do it in batches as needed, then place the tomato slices in your air fryer basket in a single layer and spritz with cooking spray.

6. Cook for about 8 to 12 minutes turning halfway (until golden brown), spritzing with additional cooking spray.

7. When the time is up, remove and keep warm, repeat the process with the remaining tomato slices.

8. Meanwhile, mix together mayonnaise, green onions and dill. Layer each of four slices of bread with two bacon strips, one lettuce leaf and two tomato slices.

9. Spread the mayonnaise mixture over the remaining slices of bread and place over top.

10. Serve immediately and enjoy!

CHAPTER 2: LUNCH & DINNER RECIPES

Flourless Chicken Cordon Bleu

Preparation time: 5 minutes

Cooking time: 30 minutes

Total time: 35 minutes

Serves: 2 to 3 people

Recipe Ingredients:

- 2 chicken breasts
- 1 slice cheddar cheese
- 1 tablespoons of soft cheese
- 1 slice ham
- 20 g oats
- 1 small egg beaten
- 1 teaspoon of garlic puree
- 1 teaspoon of parsley
- 1 tablespoon of tarragon
- 1 tablespoon of thyme
- Salt & pepper

Cooking Instructions:

1. First preheat the air fryer to 180°c. Place the chicken breasts on a chopping board.

2. Chop them at a side angle to right near to the corner so that you can fold them over. Then add ingredients to the Centre.

3. Sprinkle all sides of the chicken with pepper, salt and tarragon. Add the soft cheese, garlic and parsley in a mixing bowl and mix them together.

4. Place a layer of the cheese mixture in the middle along with ½ a slice each of the cheddar cheese and the ham.

5. Press down on the chicken so that it looks like it is sealed with a layer of filling inside it.

6. Then add the egg in one small bowl and in another add the blended oats. Add thyme in the blended oats bowl and mix well.

7. First roll the chicken in the oats, then the egg and back in the oats. Place the chicken pieces on a baking sheet in the air fryer.

8. Set to cook for 30 minutes at 180°c. After 20 minutes turn it over so that both sides have the chance to be crispy.

9. After the 30 minutes. Serve with new potatoes and enjoy!

Hot Dogs

Preparation time: 3 minutes

Cooking time: 7 minutes

Total time: 10 minutes

Serves: 2

Recipe Ingredients:

2 hot dogs

2 hot dog buns

2 tbsp. of grated cheese (if desired)

Cooking Instructions:

1. First preheat your air fryer to 390° for 4 minutes. Then place two hot dogs into your Air fryer.

2. Set to cook for about 5 minutes. When the time is up, remove the hot dog from the Air fryer.

3. Place the hot dog on a bun, add cheese if desired. Place dressed hot dog into the air fryer.

4. Set to cook for an additional 2 minutes. When the time is up.

5. Serve and enjoy!

Herb and Cheese-Stuffed Burgers

Total time: 40 minutes

Preparation time: 20 minutes

Cooking time: 20 minutes/batch

Serves: 3 to 4 people

Recipe Ingredients:

- ¼ cup of cubed cheddar cheese
- 2 green onions (thinly sliced)
- 2 tbsp. of minced fresh parsley
- 3 tsp. of Dijon mustard, divided
- 3 tbsp. of dry bread crumbs
- 2 tbsp. of ketchup
- ½ tsp. of salt
- ½ tsp. of dried rosemary, crushed
- ¼ tsp. of dried sage leaves
- 1 lb. lean ground beef (90% lean)
- 4 hamburger buns, split
- (Optional toppings) lettuce leaves and tomato slices

Cooking Instructions:

1. First preheat your Air fryer to 375°. Then mix cheddar cheese, green onions, parsley and 1 tsp. of mustard in a small bowl.

2. Mix the bread crumbs, ketchup, seasonings and remaining mustard in another bowl.

3. Add beef to bread crumb mixture and mix lightly but thoroughly. Shape mixture into eight thin patties.

4. Then Spoon the cheese mixture onto the Centre of four patties. Top with remaining patties, pressing edges together firmly.

5. Seal completely. Place burgers in a single layer in your Air fryer basket. Working in batches as needed.

6. Air-fry for about 10 minutes, flip and continue cooking until your thermometer reads 160°, around 8 to 10 minutes longer.

7. Serve and enjoy!

Chicken Breast

Preparation time: 15 minutes

Cooking time: 10 minutes

Total time: 20 minutes

Serves: 3 to 4 people

Recipe Ingredients:

- 1 pound of boneless skinless chicken breasts
- 1 tbsp. of olive oil

Breading:

- ¼ cup of bread crumbs
- ½ tsp. of salt
- ¼ tsp. of black pepper
- ½ tsp. of paprika
- 1/8 tsp. of garlic powder
- 1/8 tsp. of onion powder
- 1/16 tsp. of cayenne pepper

Cooking Instructions:

1. First preheat your Air fryer to 390°F. Then slice the chicken breasts in half to make two thin chicken breast halves from each.

2. Use olive oil to brush each side lightly. Stir the breading ingredients together.

3. Dredge the chicken breasts in the breading multiple times until they are coated entirely.

4. Shake off excess breading, place them in your Air fryer (2 chicken breast halves at a time).

5. Set to cook for about 4 minutes, flip, then two more minutes. Cook time depends on the size and thickness of the chicken breasts you used.

6. So, cut one in half to see if they are done.

7. Serve and enjoy!

KFC Chicken Strips

Preparation time: 10 minutes

Cooking time: 12 minutes

Total time: 22 minutes

Serves: 7 to 8 people

Recipe Ingredients:

- 1 chicken breast (chopped into strips)
- 15 ml desiccated coconut
- 15 ml plain oats
- 5 ml KFC spice blend
- 75 ml bread crumbs
- 50 g plain flour
- 1 small egg beaten
- Salt & pepper

Cooking Instructions:

1. First chop up the chicken breast into strips. Add the coconut, oats, KFC spice blend, bread crumbs, salt and pepper together in one bowl.

2. Add the egg in another bowl and in another bowl add your plain flour. Put your strips in the plain flour, then in the egg and finally in the spicy layer.

3. Place them in your Air fryer at 180°c. Set to cook for about 8 minutes and then cook for a further 4 minutes on 160c because of the Centre of the chicken.

4. When the time is up, serve and enjoy!

Rotisserie Style Whole Chicken

Preparation time: 5 minutes

Cooking time: 1 hour

Resting time: 10 minutes

Total time: 1 hour 5 minutes

Serves: 3 to 4 people

Recipe Ingredients:

- 1 whole chicken cleaned and blotted dry
- 2 tbsp. of Ghee, coconut or olive oil
- 1 tbsp. of TOG house seasoning

Cooking Instructions:

1. Remove giblet packet from chicken and pat dry. Rub ghee/oil all over the chicken and season thoroughly.

2. Then place chicken, breast side down into your Air fryer. Set to cook at 350° for about 30 minutes.

3. Flip chicken over and set to cook for 350° for an additional 30 minutes.

4. When the time is up, allow it to rest for about 10 minutes.

5. Serve immediately and enjoy!

Fried Chicken

Preparation time: 5 minutes

Cooking time: 25 minutes

Total time: 30 minutes

Serves: 3 to 4 people

Recipe Ingredients:

- ½ cup all-purpose flour
- 1 egg beaten
- 4 small chicken thighs
- 1½ tablespoons of old bay Cajun seasoning
- 1 teaspoon of seasoning salt

Cooking Instructions:

1. First heat your Air fryer to 390° and whisk together the flour, salt and the Old Bay.

2. Dredge the chicken through the flour mixture, then into the egg, then back into the flour mixture.

3. Shake off excess flour and place the chicken thighs into the bottom of your Air fryer cooking compartment.

4. Set to cook for about 25 minutes. When the time is up, remove and serve immediately.

Air-Fried Buttermilk Chicken

Recipe Ingredients:

- 800g store-bought chicken thighs (skin on, bone in)

For Marinade:

- 2 cups of buttermilk
- 2 tsp. of salt
- 2 tsp. of black pepper
- 1 tsp. of cayenne pepper (We used paprika powder)
- Seasoned flour
- 2 cups all-purpose flour
- 1 tbsp. of baking powder
- 1 tbsp. of garlic powder
- 1 tbsp. of paprika powder
- 1 tsp. of salt

Cooking Instructions:

1. First rinse the chicken thighs to remove any obvious fat and residue.

2. Pat dry the chicken with paper towels. In a large bowl, toss together chicken pieces, black pepper, paprika and salt to coat.

3. Then pour the buttermilk over until chicken is coated thoroughly. Refrigerated for about 6 hours or overnight.

4. Preheat your Air fryer at 180°C. Combine the flour, baking powder, paprika and salt and pepper together in a separate mixing bowl.

5. Remove the chicken from the buttermilk and dredge in seasoned flour (Do it 1 piece at a time).

6. Shake off any excess flour. Transfer the chicken to a plate and arrange the chicken one layer on the fryer basket, skin side up.

7. Slide the basket into your Air fryer. Set to air fry for about 8 minutes. After the 8 minutes, pull out the tray, turn chicken pieces over.

8. Set to Air-fry for another 10 minutes. Allow to drain on paper towels.

9. Serve and enjoy!

6 Minute Pita Bread Cheese Pizza

Recipe Ingredients:

- 1 pita bread
- 1 tbsp. of pizza sauce
- ¼ cup of mozarella cheese
- 1 drizzle extra virgin olive oil
- 1 stainless steel short legged trivet

Toppings:

- 7 slices Pepperoni or more
- ¼ cup of sausage
- 1 tbsp. of onion (sliced thin)
- ½ tsp. of fresh garlic, minced

Cooking Instructions:

1. Use a spoon and swirl pizza sauce on to pita bread.

2. Then add your favorite toppings and cheese, add a little drizzle of extra virgin olive oil over the top of the pizza.

3. Place pita bread in your Air fryer and place a Trivet over pita bread. Set timer to cook at 350°F for about 6 minutes.

4. When the time is up, remove it from your Air fryer carefully.

5. Cut and serve.

Simple Grilled American Cheese Sandwich

Preparation time: 2 minutes

Cooking time: 8 minutes

Total time: 10 minutes

Serves: 1

Recipe Ingredients:

- 2 slices of sandwich bread
- 2 to 3 slices of cheddar cheese
- 2 tsp. of butter or mayonnaise

Cooking Instructions:

1. Place cheese between bread slices.

2. Butter the outside of both slices of the bread.

3. Place in your Air fryer. Set timer to cook at 370° for about 8 minutes.

4. Flip, halfway through. When the time is up.

5. Serve and enjoy!

Leftover Turkey & Cheese Calzone

Preparation time: 10 minutes

Cooking time: 10 minutes

Total time: 20 minutes

Serves: 3 to 4 people

Recipe Ingredients:

- Homemade pizza dough
- 4 tbsp. of Homemade tomato sauce
- Leftover turkey brown meat, shredded
- 100 g cheddar cheese
- 25 g mozzarella cheese grated
- 25 g back bacon diced
- 1 large egg beaten
- 1 tablespoon of tomato puree
- 1 teaspoon of oregano
- 1 teaspoon of basil
- 1 teaspoon of thyme
- Salt & pepper

Cooking Instructions:

1. preheat the Air fryer to 180°c. Roll out the pizza dough so that they are the size of small pizzas.

2. Add together all the seasonings including the tomato sauce and puree in a small mixing bowl.

3. Use a cooking brush to add a layer of tomato sauce to the pizza bases. Ensure that it doesn't actually touch the edge with a 1cm space.

4. Layer up the pizza with the turkey, bacon and cheese to one side. With the 1cm gap around the pizza base.

5. Then use a cooking brush to brush with beaten egg. After brushing, fold the pizza base over so that it resembles an uncooked Cornish pasty.

6. Brush all area that is now visible of the pizza dough, brush with more egg. Place in your Air fryer, set timer to cook for about 10 minutes at 180°c.

7. After the 10 minutes, serve immediately and enjoy!

Midnight Nutella Banana Sandwich

Preparation time: 5 minutes

Cooking time: 8 minutes

Total time: 13 minutes

Serves: 2 people

Recipe Ingredients:

- Butter, softened
- 4 slices of white bread
- ¼ cup of chocolate hazelnut spread
- 1 banana

Cooking Instructions:

1. Start by heating your Air fryer to 370°F. Then spread the softened butter on one side of all the slices of bread.

2. Place the bread slices, buttered side down on the counter. Spread the chocolate hazelnut spread on the other side of the bread slices.

3. Cut the banana in half, slice each half into three slices lengthwise. Place the banana slices on two slices of bread.

4. Top with the remaining slices of bread to make two sandwiches. Then cut the sandwiches in half (triangles or rectangles).

5. Transfer the sandwiches to your Air fryer. Set timer to Air-fry at 370°F for about 5 minutes.

6. After the 5 minutes, flip the sandwiches over and air-fry for another 2 to 3 minutes.

7. When the time is up, allow the sandwiches to cool slightly.

8. Serve and enjoy!

Pickle-Brined Fried Chicken

Serves: 3 to 4 people

Recipe Ingredients:

- 4 chicken legs (bone-in and skin-on), cut into drumsticks and thighs (3½ lb.)
- Pickle juice from a 24-oz jar of kosher dill pickles
- ½ cup of flour
- Salt and freshly ground black pepper
- 2 eggs
- 2 tbsp. of vegetable
- 1 cup fine breadcrumbs
- 1 tsp. of salt
- 1 tsp. of freshly ground black pepper
- ½ tsp. of ground paprika
- ⅛ tsp. of cayenne pepper
- vegetable or canola oil in a spray bottle

Cooking Instructions:

1. In a shallow dish, place the chicken and pour the pickle juice over the top.

2. Cover and transfer chicken to the refrigerator to brine in the pickle juice for about 4 to 9 hours.

3. After refrigerating for hours, remove the chicken from your refrigerator to let it come to room temperature.

4. Set up a dredging station and place the flour in a shallow dish. Season well with salt and freshly ground black pepper.

5. In a second shallow dish, whisk the eggs and the vegetable oil together. In a third shallow dish.

6. Combine the breadcrumbs, salt, pepper, paprika and cayenne pepper. Then preheat your Air fryer to 370°F.

7. Carefully remove the chicken from pickle brine and gently dry it with a clean kitchen towel.

8. First dredge each piece of chicken in the flour and dip it into the egg mixture (Do 1 piece at a time).

9. Finally press it into the breadcrumb mixture to coat all sides of the chicken.

10. Place the breaded chicken on a plate and spray each piece all over with vegetable oil.

11. Air-fry the chicken (You have to do it in two batches). Place two chicken thighs and two drumsticks into your Air fryer basket.

12. Set timer to Air-fry for about 10 minutes. After the 10 minutes, gently turn the chicken pieces over and air fry for another 10 minutes.

13. After the 10 minutes, carefully remove the chicken pieces and let them rest on a plate (Do not cover).

14. Repeat the process with the second batch of chicken. Lower the temperature of your Air fryer to 340°F.

15. Place the first batch of chicken on top of the second batch already in the basket, Air-fry for an additional 7 minutes.

16. When the time is up, serve immediately and enjoy!

Whole30 Lemon Pepper Chicken

Preparation time: 3 minutes

Cooking time: 15 minutes

Total time: 18 minutes

Serves: 1

Recipe Ingredients:

- 1 chicken breast
- 2 lemons rind and juice
- 1 tablespoon of chicken seasoning
- 1 teaspoon of garlic puree
- Handful black peppercorns
- Salt & pepper to taste

Cooking Instructions:

1. Start by heating your Air fryer to 180°c. Set up your work station.

2. Place a large sheet of silver foil on the work top, then add all the seasonings to it and the lemon rind.

3. Place the chicken breasts onto a chopping board, trim off any fatty bits and any little bones on the chicken breast.

4. Season each side with salt and pepper. Rub the chicken seasoning into both sides so that it is slightly a different color.

5. Then place the chicken breast in the silver foil sheet and rub it well so that it is fully seasoned.

6. Seal it up very tight. Give it a slap with a rolling pin so that it will flatten it out and release more flavor.

7. Place it in your Air fryer for about 15 minutes. Check to see if it is fully cooked in the middle before serving.

8. When the time is up, serve immediately and enjoy!

Thanksgiving Turkey

Preparation time: 10 minutes

Cooking time: 35 minutes

Overall time: 45 minutes

Serves: 3 to 4 people

Recipe Ingredients:

- 2 pounds of turkey breast
- Kosher salt
- Freshly ground black pepper
- 1 teaspoon of freshly chopped thyme
- 1 teaspoon of freshly chopped rosemary
- 1 teaspoon of freshly chopped sage
- ¼ cup of maple syrup
- 2 tablespoons of Dijon mustard
- 1 tablespoon of butter, melted

Cooking Instructions:

1. Start by seasoning the turkey breast generously with salt and pepper, rub the breast all over with fresh herbs.

2. Then place in your Air fryer and fry at 390° for about 30 to 35 minutes. Whisk together maple syrup, Dijon, and melted butter in a small bowl.

3. When the time is up, carefully remove turkey from the Air fryer. Brush mixture all over.

4. Return it to your Air fryer and fry at 330° until caramelized, for about 2 minutes.

5. After the 2 minutes, Let rest for about 15 minutes before slicing.

6. Serve and enjoy!

Air Fried Chicken Tenders

Preparation time: 10 minutes

Cooking time: 10 minutes

Overall time: 20 minutes

Recipe Ingredients:

- 12 ounces of chicken breasts
- 1 egg white
- 1/8 cup of flour
- 35g panko bread crumbs
- Salt and pepper

Cooking Instructions:

1. Start by trimming the chicken breast of any excess fat and bones, cut into tenders.

2. After cutting, season each side with salt and pepper. Then dip chicken tenders accordingly, dip into flour, egg whites, then panko bread crumbs.

3. Place into your Air fryer basket and spray with olive spray. Set timer to cook at 350° for about 10 minutes or until cooked through

4. When the time is up, serve and enjoy!

CHAPTER 3: SIDE DISH RECIPES

Garlic-Rosemary Brussels Sprouts

Overall time: 30 minutes

Serves: 3 to 4 people

Recipe Ingredients:

- 3 tbsp. of olive oil
- 2 garlic cloves, minced
- ½ tsp. of salt
- ¼ tsp. of pepper
- 1 lb. of brussels sprouts (trimmed and halved)
- ½ cup of panko (Japanese) bread crumbs
- 1½ tsp. of minced fresh rosemary

Cooking Instructions:

1. Preheat your Air fryer to 350° and place the first four ingredients in a small microwave-safe bowl.

2. Microwave on high for about 30 seconds. Toss brussels sprouts with 2 tbsp. of oil mixture.

3. Then place all the Brussels sprouts in your Air fryer basket. Set timer to cook for about 4 to 5 minutes.

4. Give sprouts a good stir. Continue to air fry, stirring every 4 to 5 minutes, until sprouts are nearing desired tenderness and are lightly browned, about 8 minutes.

5. Toss bread crumbs with rosemary and remaining oil mixture. Sprinkle over sprouts.

6. Continue cooking until crumbs are browned and sprouts are tender, for about 3 to 5 minutes.

7. When the time is up, serve immediately and enjoy!

Thyme Garlic Tomatoes

Serves: 3 to 4 people

Recipe Ingredients:

- 4 Roma tomatoes
- 1 tbsp. of olive oil
- A pinch of salt
- Freshly ground black pepper
- 1 clove garlic, minced
- ½ tsp. of dried thyme

Cooking Instructions:

1. Preheat your Air Fryer to about 390°F.

2. Use a sharp knife to cut the tomatoes in half, scoop out the seeds and any pithy parts with your fingers.

3. In a medium bowl, place the tomatoes and toss it with the olive oil, salt, pepper, garlic and thyme.

4. Transfer the tomatoes to your Air Fryer, cut side up. Set your Air fryer to Air fry the tomatoes for about 15 minutes at 390°F.

5. When the edges start to brown, allow the tomatoes to cool to an edible temperature for a few minutes.

6. Serve with pastas, on top of crostini.

7. Serve and enjoy!

Roasted Vegetable Pasta Salad

Serves: 6 to 8

Ingredients:

- 1 orange pepper, large chunks
- 1 green pepper, large chunks
- 1 red pepper, large chunks
- 1 zucchini, sliced in half moons
- 1 yellow squash, sliced in half moons
- 1 red onion, sliced
- 4 oz. of brown mushrooms, halved
- 1 tsp. of Italian seasoning
- A pinch of salt
- Fresh ground black pepper
- 1 lb. of penne rigate or rigatoni, cooked
- 1 cup of grape tomatoes, halved
- ½ cup of pitted Kalamata olives, halved
- 3 tbsp. of balsamic vinegar
- ¼ cup of olive oil
- 2 tbsp. of chopped fresh basil

Cooking Instructions:

1. Start by Preheating your Air fryer to 380°F.

2. In a large bowl, place the peppers, zucchini, yellow squash, red onion and mushrooms and drizzle it with a little bit of olive oil.

3. Toss it very well to coat evenly. Add the Italian seasoning and add salt and pepper into the mixture. Set your Air fryer to Air-fry for about 12 to 15 minutes.

4. Shake the basket halfway through the cooking time to evenly roast vegetables.

5. In a separate large bowl, combine together the cooked pasta, roasted vegetables tomatoes and olives and mix thoroughly to combine.

6. Add the balsamic vinegar and toss them very well. Add more olive oil to evenly coat everything.

7. Season the contents with more salt and freshly ground black pepper to taste. Place the salad in the refrigerate until you are ready to serve.

8. Stir in the fresh basil right before serving.

9. Serve and enjoy!

Baked Zucchini Fries

Preparation time: 10 minutes

Cooking time: 20 minutes

Overall time: 30 minutes

Recipe Ingredients:

- 3 medium zucchini sliced into sticks
- 2 large egg white
- ½ cup of seasoned bread crumbs
- 2 tablespoons of grated Parmesan cheese
- Cooking spray
- ¼ teaspoon of garlic powder
- salt & pepper to taste

Cooking Instructions:

1. Preheat oven to 425° and place a cooling rack inside a baking sheet. Coat rack with cooking spray and set aside.

2. Beat egg whites and season with salt and pepper in a small mixing bowl. In another mixing bowl.

3. Place breadcrumbs, garlic powder and cheese. mix well to combine. Then dip zucchini sticks into eggs then into bread crumb and cheese mixture.

4. Set the breaded zucchini in a single layer onto the cooling rack, spray more cooking spray on top.

5. Bake at 425° for about 15 to 20 minutes (Until golden brown). When the time is up.

6. Serve with Ranch or Marinara sauce for dipping.

Healthy Mediterranean vegetables

Preparation time: 5 minutes

Cooking time: 20 minutes

Total time: 25 minutes

Serves: 3 to 4 people

Recipe Ingredients:

- 50 g cherry tomatoes
- 1 large courgette
- 1 green pepper
- 1 large parsnip
- 1 medium carrot
- 1 tsp. of mixed herbs
- 2 tablespoons of honey
- 1 teaspoon of mustard
- 2 teaspoons of garlic puree
- 6 tablespoon of olive oil
- Salt & pepper

Cooking Instructions:

1. In the bottom of the Air fryer, (chopping as you go) slice up the courgette and green pepper.

2. Peel and dice the parsnip and carrot. Add the cherry tomatoes whole while still on the vine for extra flavor.

3. Drizzle with 3 tbsp. of olive oil. Set timer to cook for about 15 minutes at 180°C.

4. In the meantime, mix up the remaining ingredients into an Air fryer safe baking dish.

5. Once the vegetables are done, carefully transfer them from the bottom of the Air fryer into the baking dish.

6. Shake well so that all the vegetables are covered in the marinade. Sprinkle with a little more salt and pepper.

7. Set timer to cook for about 5 minutes at 200°C. when the time is up.

8. Serve and enjoy!

Cauliflower Tater Tots

Serves: 6 to 8 people

Recipe Ingredients:

- 1 head of cauliflower
- 2 eggs
- ¼ cup of all-purpose flour
- ½ cup of grated Parmesan cheese
- 1 tsp. of salt
- Freshly ground black pepper
- Oil, in a spray bottle

Cooking Instructions:

1. Using a box grater or food processor, grate the head of the cauliflower.

2. Put the chopped cauliflower in the center of a clean kitchen towel and twist the towel tightly to squeeze all the water out of the cauliflower.

3. In a large bowl, place the squeezed cauliflower and add the eggs, flour, Parmesan cheese, salt and freshly ground black pepper.

4. Shape the cauliflower into small cylinders or "tater tot" shapes, rolling roughly 1 tbsp. of the mixture at a time.

5. Place the tots on a cookie sheet lined or clean surface with paper towel to absorb any residual moisture.

6. Generously spray the cauliflower tots with the oil. Preheat your Air fryer to 400°F.

7. Set your Air fryer to cook the tots at 400°F, one layer at a time for about 10 minutes.

8. Shake them over for the last few minutes of the cooking process for even browning.

9. Generously season the tots with salt and black pepper to taste.

10. Serve warm with your favorite dipping sauce.

11. Serve and enjoy!

Mac and Cheese

Recipe Ingredients

- 1 cup of elbow macaroni
- ½ cup of broccoli OR cauliflower (equal size small florets)
- ½ cup of milk (Warmed)
- 1½ of cup of cheddar cheese (grated)
- Salt & pepper
- 1 tablespoon of parmesan cheese (grated)

Cooking Instructions:

1. First preheat your Air fryer at 200°C. Bring a pot of water to boil over high heat, reduce to medium heat.

2. Add in macaroni and vegetables. Simmer until macaroni is al dente and vegetables are tender but not mushy, around 7 to 10 minutes.

3. Drain pasta and vegetables and return them to the pot. Add the milk and cheddar cheese to the macaroni and vegetables.

4. Toss to combine. After tossing, season with pepper and salt. Then pour pasta mixture into an ovenproof dish.

5. Sprinkle the Parmesan cheese over the top. Place the dish on the Air fryer basket.

6. Set temperature to 180°C and bake for about 15 minutes (the pasta will be bubbling).

7. When the time is up, allow to sit for about 5 to 10 minutes in the Air fryer.

8. Serve and enjoy!

Breaded mushrooms

Recipe Ingredients:

- 250g of button mushrooms
- Flour
- 1 egg
- Breadcrumbs
- 80g of finely grated Parmigiano Reggiano cheese
- Salt and pepper

Cooking Instructions:

1. In a medium mixing bowl, mix the breadcrumbs with the Parmigiano cheese and place to one side.

2. Beat the egg in a separate mixing bowl. Pat dry the mushrooms with kitchen paper.

3. Roll the mushrooms in the flour, then dip the mushrooms in the egg. Finally dip the mushrooms in the breadcrumbs/cheese mixture.

4. Make sure the mushrooms are evenly coated. Adjust timer to cook at 180°C for about 7 minutes.

5. Shake once while cooking. After the minutes. Serve warm with your favorite dipping sauce.

6. Serve and enjoy!

Lemony Green Beans

Serves: 3-4

Recipe Ingredients:

- 1 pound of green beans (washed and destemmed)
- 1 lemon
- Pinch of salt
- Black pepper to taste
- ¼ tsp. of oil

Recipe Ingredients:

1. Start by putting green beans in your Air fryer.

2. Add a few squeezes of lemon. Then add salt and pepper.

3. Drizzle oil over the top. Set to cook at 400° for about 10 to 12 minutes.

4. When the time is up, serve and enjoy!

Hamburger Hamlet Zucchini Zircles

Preparation time: 15 minutes

Cooking time: 8 minutes

Total time: 23 minutes

Serves: 3 to 4 people

Recipe Ingredients:

- 3 large Zucchini
- ¾ cup of milk
- ½ cup All Purpose Flour
- 1 cup of seasoned dry Italian breadcrumbs
- ½ cup of powdered sugar
- 1 cup of Hamburger hamlet's secret apricot sauce
- Tools
- Oil mister
- 1 half cookie sheet
- 1 wire baking rack

Cooking Instructions:

1. Line a cookie sheet with paper towels. Wash and dry Zucchini.

2. Cut Zucchini (about ¼ inch thick, like poker chips) place on lined cookie sheet.

3. set up 3 shallow bowls, place flour in one, milk in the next and seasoned bread crumbs in the third.

4. Use one dry hand to coat Zucchini in flour, shake off excess and drop into milk.

5. Flip with a fork and then place Zucchini in bowl with breadcrumbs. With other dry hand, coat Zucchini generously and place onto wire baking rack.

6. Gently place Zucchini Zircles in a single layer, place it in prepared/greased Air fryer basket.

7. Use an oil mister to spray well with Oil. Set to cook at 390°F for about 8 minutes. Carefully flip one-half way through.

8. Carefully remove it from Air fryer, sprinkle with Powdered Sugar.

9. Serve with hamburger hamlet's secret apricot sauce.

10. Serve and enjoy!

Shoestring Air-Fried Carrots

Recipe Ingredients:

- 1 bag (10 oz.) of julienned carrots
- 1 tbsp. of olive oil
- Salt and pepper
- Apple cider vinegar in a spray bottle
- 1 tsp. of orange zest

Cooking Instructions:

1. Mix the carrots with the olive oil, coating them lightly in a medium mixing bowl.

2. Coat all pieces of carrots and season with salt and pepper. Place the carrots in your Air fryer. Adjust temperature to 390°F and cook for about 13 to 16 minutes.

3. Mix them around every few minutes. Remove when they start to get nicely brown.

4. When the time is up, transfer them to a serving bowl. Add orange zest, spray a little apple cider vinegar.

5. Taste and season with more salt and pepper if needed.

6. Serve immediately and enjoy!

Roasted Corn

Recipe Ingredients:

- 4 fresh ears of corn
- 2-3 tsp. of vegetable oil
- Salt and pepper to taste

Cooking Instructions:

1. Start by removing husks from corn, wash in clean water and pat dry.

2. If the corn is too big, cut the corn to fit in your Air fryer basket. Drizzle vegetable oil over the corn.

3. Cover the corn well with the vegetable oil and season with salt and pepper.

4. Adjust temperature to 400°F and cook for about 10 minutes.

5. When the time is up, serve and enjoy!

Garlic and Vermouth Roasted Mushrooms

Preparation time: 10 minutes

Cooking time: 30 minutes

Overall time: 40 minutes

Serves: 3 to 4 people

Recipe Ingredients:

- 1 kg mushrooms (fresh 2 lb.)
- 1 tablespoons of duck fat (or goose fat)
- ½ tsp. of garlic powder
- 2 tsp. of herbes de provence
- 2 tbsp. of white vermouth (aka French vermouth)

Cooking Instructions:

1. Start by washing the mushrooms, spin dry in a salad spinner. Quarter them and reserve aside.

2. Add the duck fat, the garlic powder, and the herbes de provence in the pan of your paddle-type.

3. Heat for about 2 minutes. Stir with a wooden spoon if it clumped. Then add the mushrooms.

4. Set to cook for about 25 minutes. After the 25 minutes, add the white vermouth.

5. Set timer to cook for another 5 minutes.

6. When the time is up, serve and enjoy.

CHAPTER 4: SNACK & APPETIZERS RECIPES

Honey Garlic Chicken Wings

Preparation time: 10 minutes

Cooking time: 35 minutes

Overall time: 45 minutes

Serves: 2

Recipes Ingredients:

- 16 Pieces of chicken wings
- ¾ cup of potato starch
- ¼ cup of clover honey
- ¼ cup of butter
- 4 tbsp. of fresh garlic, minced
- ½ tsp. of kosher salt
- 1/8 cup of fresh water (or more as needed)

Cooking Instructions:

1. Rinse and dry chicken wings. In a medium bowl, add in the potato starch and coat chicken wings thoroughly.

2. Then add the coated chicken wings to your Air fryer. Set timer to cook at 380°F for about 25 minutes.

3. Ensure to shake the basket every 5 minutes. After the 25 minutes, set timer to cook at 400°F for about 5 to 10 minutes.

4. All skin on all wings will be very dry and crisp. Heat a small stainless-steel saucepan on low heat.

5. Melt butter and then add garlic. Sauté the garlic for about 5 minutes. Add honey and salt, simmer on low for 20 minutes, stirring every few minutes.

6. Add a few drops of water after 15 minutes to keep Sauce from hardening. When the time is up.

7. Carefully remove the chicken wings from your Air fryer and pour over the sauce.

8. Serve and enjoy!

Italian Bruschetta

Preparation time: 5 minutes

Cooking time: 6 minutes

Overall time: 11 minutes

Recipe Ingredients:

- Medium ciabatta
- 30 grams of Italian cheese
- 1 medium tomato, diced
- 1 tbsp. of garlic puree
- 3 tbsp. of olive oil
- 1 tbsp. of oregano
- Fresh basil
- A pinch of salt
- Freshly ground pepper

Cooking Instructions:

1. Start by preheating your Air fryer to 360°F.

2. Dice the tomato and generously season with the oregano, salt and pepper to taste.

3. In a medium bowl, mix together the garlic puree and olive oil. Add in the remaining seasonings and stir.

4. Cut up the ciabatta into medium slices and use a pastry brush to brush one side with the garlic and oil mix.

5. Place it in a grill pan and add it into the Air fryer. Place the oil side down, set your Air fryer to cook for about 4 minutes at 360°F.

6. Turn the slice over and add the cheese, tomato mix and the basil. Set your Air fryer to cook it for additional 2 minutes at 390°F.

7. When the time is up, serve hot and enjoy!

Buffalo Cauliflower

Preparation time: 5 minutes

Cooking time: 15 minutes

Total time: 20 minutes

Serves: 3 to 4 people

Recipe Ingredients:

For the Cauliflower:

- 4 cups of cauliflower florets (Each one should be approximately the size of two baby carrots)
- 1 cup of panko breadcrumbs mixed with 1 tsp. of sea salt

For the Buffalo Coating:

- ¼ cup of melted vegan butter - ¼ cup after melting
- ¼ cup of vegan Buffalo sauce - check the ingredients for butter. (We used Frank's Red Hot)

For Dipping:

- vegan mayo - Cashew Ranch, or your favorite creamy salad dressing

Cooking Instructions:

1. Melt vegan butter in a mug in the microwave, whisk in the buffalo sauce.

2. Holding by the stem and dip each floret in the butter/buffalo mixture. Coat the floret in the sauce.

3. Hold the floret over the mug until it stops dripping. A few drips are OK, but if it's raining sauce, the panko is going to get clumpy and stop sticking as well.

4. Dredge the dipped floret in the panko/salt mixture and coat the floret in the mixture as much as you like.

5. Place in your Air fryer and Air fry at 350°F for about 14 to 17 minutes. Shake few times during cooking process.

6. Check their progress when you shake. Your cauliflower is done when the florets are a little bit browned.

7. Serve with your dipping sauce of choice. Serve and enjoy!

Reheat Pizza

Preparation time: 2 minutes

Cooking time: 5 minutes

Overall time: 7 minutes

Recipe Ingredient:

- 1 leftover pizza slice

Cooking Instructions:

1. Start by preheating your Air fryer to 320°F.

2. Place the 1 leftover pizza slice into your Air Fryer basket.

3. Set your Air fryer to cook the pizza for about 5 minutes.

4. After the 5 minutes, serve and enjoy!

Grilled Brie with Roasted Cherry Tomatoes

Serves: 6 to 8 people

Recipe Ingredients:

- 2 pints of red and yellow cherry tomatoes
- 1 tbsp. of olive oil
- 1 tsp. of balsamic vinegar
- 1 tsp. of salt
- Freshly ground black pepper
- 1 tbsp. of chopped fresh parley
- 1 (8-oz.) wheel of Brie cheese
- Olive oil
- ½ tsp. of Italian seasoning, optional
- 1 loaf of ciabatta bread or baguette
- 1 tablespoon of chopped fresh basil
- Balsamic glaze, (Optional)

Cooking Instructions:

1. Start by preheating your Air Fryer to 225°F.

2. In a medium bowl, toss the cherry tomatoes with the olive oil, balsamic vinegar, salt and pepper.

3. Place the cherry tomatoes into your Air fryer basket. Set your Air fryer to air-fry for about 45 minutes, tossing them at least 3 times during the cooking time.

4. The tomatoes will be soft and some of them will burst open. Allow the tomatoes to cool down a little and stir in the fresh parsley.

5. Preheat your outdoor grill to medium-low heat. Brush both sides of the Brie wheel with the olive oil and sprinkle it with the Italian seasoning, if desired.

6. Slice the bread into ½ inch slices and slice the baguette on the bias if desired. Brush one side of the bread with the olive oil.

7. Grill the both sides of the bread until it is lightly browned. Set the bread aside. Put the Brie wheel directly on the grill grate.

8. Once the Brie has grill marks on the bottom after about 3 minutes, flip it over and mark the second side.

9. Carefully lower the flame on the grill and allow the Brie to heat through until it is soft and melted, for additional 5 to 10 minutes.

10. The Brie should appear soft to the touch and start to expand a little. Gently remove the Brie before the rind cracks and the cheese starts to leak out.

11. Then, carefully transfer the wheel to your serving platter and drizzle the Brie with balsamic glaze if desired and sprinkle the basil on top.

12. Serve warm with the toasted bread slices and roasted tomatoes.

13. Serve and enjoy!

Mozzarella Sticks

Serves: 3 to 4 people

Recipe Ingredients:

- 1 lb. of Mozzarella cheese, block
- 2 eggs
- 3 tbsp. of milk, nonfat
- 0.25 cup of flour, white
- 1 cup of bread crumbs, plain

Cooking Instructions:

1. Start by cutting cheese into 3 x ½ inch sticks. In a medium bowl, place bread crumbs.

2. Place flour in a mixing bowl. In a separate bowl, mix the egg and milk together.

3. Dip cheese sticks in flour, then egg, and finally bread crumbs. Lay breaded sticks on a at cookie sheet.

4. Freeze in freezer until solid for about 1 to 2 minutes. Place small batches of breaded sticks into the Fry Basket (do not overcrowd Air fryer).

5. Select the M Button and scroll to the French fries Icon. Now select the Power Button & set timer to cook at 400°F for about 12 minutes.

6. When the time is up, serve and enjoy!

Sweet and Salty Snack Mix

Makes: 10 cups

Recipe Ingredients:

- ½ cup of honey
- 3 tbsp. of butter, melted
- 1 teaspoon of salt
- 2 cups of sesame sticks
- 1 cup pepitas or pumpkin seeds
- 2 cups of granola
- 1 cup of cashews
- 2 cups of crispy corn puff cereal
- 2 cups of mini pretzel crisps

Cooking Instructions:

1. In a medium bowl, combine the honey, butter, and salt together. Stir everything together to combine.

2. In a large bowl, combine together the sesame sticks, pepitas, granola, cashews, corn puff cereal, and pretzel crisps.

3. Pour honey mixture over the top and toss everything to combine evenly. Preheat your Air Fryer to 370°F.

4. Air fry the snack mix in two batches and place half of the mixture in the air fryer basket.

5. Set your Air fryer to air-fry the snack mixes for about 10 to 12 minutes, or until the snack mix is lightly toasted.

6. Shake the basket several times throughout the cooking process to cook evenly. Place the snack mix to a cookie sheet and allow them to cool completely.

7. Store in an airtight container for up to one week or serve immediately.

8. Serve and enjoy!

Charred Shishito Peppers

Serves: 3 to 4 people

Ingredients:

- 20 Shishido peppers, about 6 oz.
- 1 tsp. of vegetable oil
- Coarse sea salt
- 1 lemon

Cooking Instructions:

1. Start by preheating your Air fryer to 390°F. In a medium bowl, toss the Shishido peppers with the oil and salt.

2. Set your Air fryer to air fry at 390°F for about 5 minutes, shaking the basket once to cook evenly during cooking.

3. Turn out the peppers from the bowl. squeeze some lemon juice on them and season with the coarse sea salt.

4. Pick up the pepper by the stem and eat the whole pepper, seeds and all.

5. Serve and enjoy!

Parmesan Dill Fried Pickle Chips

Preparation time: 14 minutes

Cooking time: 16 minutes

Overall time: 30 minutes

Serves: 3 to 4 people

Recipe Ingredients:

- 32 ounces jar whole large dill pickles
- 2 eggs
- 2/3 cup of panko bread crumbs
- 1/3 cup of grated Parmesan
- ¼ teaspoon of dried dill weed

Cooking Instructions:

1. Start by slicing the large pickles diagonally into ¼" thick slices. Place between layers of paper towels and pat dry.

2. Beat the eggs in a shallow bowl until smooth. In a resealable bag, add the Panko bread crumbs, Parmesan and dill weed.

3. Shake until well combined. Dip the pickle slices into the egg mixture (you have to do it in batches of 4 to 5 pieces).

4. Ensure to remove any excess egg, toss in the Panko mixture. Add half of the coated pickle chips into your Air fryer.

5. Bake for about 8 to 10 minutes on the highest temperature. When the time is up.

6. Remove from the Air fryer and add the remaining pickle chips. Bake for about 8 to 10 minutes.

7. When the time is up, serve with zesty ranch for dipping and enjoy!

Crispy Old Bay Chicken Wings

Preparation time: 10 minutes

Cooking time: 45 minutes

Overall time: 55 minutes

Serves: 3 to 4 people

Recipe Ingredients:

- 3 lb. of chicken wing parts
- ¾ cup of potato starch
- 1 tbsp. of Homemade old bay seasoning recipe
- ½ cup of butter
- 1 tsp. of true lemon
- Fresh lemons

Cooking Instructions:

1. Pat dry the chicken wing parts using a paper towel.

2. Mix potato starch and Homemade old bay seasoning together. Then add the chicken wings and coat the chicken wing evenly.

3. After coating the chicken wings, shake off excess potato starch. Place in your Air fryer basket.

4. Set to cook at 360°F for about 35 minutes, shaking often. When the time is up, turn temperature to 400°F and cook for additional 10 minutes, shaking often.

5. Melt the butter with true lemon and toss with hot wings. Serve wings with the remaining Lemon Butter for dipping and Lemons for squeezing.

6. Serve immediately and enjoy!

Banana Chips

Recipe Ingredients:

- Raw banana (3 to 4 pieces)
- 1 tsp of salt
- ½ tsp of Turmeric powder
- ½ tsp. of chat masala
- 1 teaspoon of oil

Cooking instructions:

1. Start by Peeling the bananas, peel the bananas and set aside.

2. Mix water, turmeric powder and salt together. Then cut slices of banana in the mixture.

3. It will prevent the bananas from turning black and also will give nice yellow colour.

4. Soak banana slices in the mixture for about 5 to 10 minutes. After soaking, drain the water and dry the chips.

5. Apply little oil on chips to avoid sticking of banana chips in your Air fryer.

6. Heat your Air fryer at 180° for about 5 minutes. Air fry the chips for about 15 min at 180°.

7. Add salt and chat masala. Store it in airtight jar and serve.

Sweet Potato Chips

Serve: 3 to 4 people

Recipe Ingredients:

- 2 medium sized sweet potatoes, thinly sliced
- ¼ cup of olive oil
- (Optional) 1 tsp. of ground cinnamon
- Salt and pepper to taste

Cooking Instructions:

1. Start by slicing the sweet potatoes very thinly. Use a mandolin or a food processor.

2. Soak the potato slices in cold water for about 30 minutes. After soaking, drain and pat dry the potato slice thoroughly.

3. Dry the potato slice completely to ensure crispy chips. Toss the potato slices with olive oil, salt, pepper and cinnamon (if using).

4. Ensure that every potato slice is coated with oil. Lightly grease your Air fry basket.

5. Air fry the potato slice in batches, Air fry the sweet potatoes at 390°F for 20 about minutes.

6. Shake the basket every 7 to 8 minutes for even cooking. If it still not crisp.

7. Air fry for additional 5 minutes. When the time is up.

8. Serve hot with ketchup and enjoy!

Apple Chips

Serves: 1

Recipe Ingredients:

- 1 medium apple
- ¼ teaspoon of cinnamon
- ¼ teaspoon of nutmeg

Cooking Instructions:

1. Start by heating your Air fryer to 375°F.

2. Slice the apple thinly using a knife. Mix together apple slices, cinnamon and nutmeg in a bowl.

3. Then transfer seasoned apple slices to you Air fryer basket in one layer.

4. Bake for about 8 minutes (flipping halfway).

5. When the time is up, serve and enjoy!

Ranch Kale Chips

Preparation time: 5 minutes

Cooking time: 5 minutes

Serves: 2

Cooking Ingredients:

- 2 tbsp. of olive oil
- 4 cups of loosely packed kale - stemmed
- 2 tsp. of vegan ranch seasoning
- 1 tbsp. of nutritional yeast flakes
- ¼ tsp. of salt

Cooking Instructions:

1. Start by tossing the oil, kale pieces, ranch seasoning, and nutritional yeast together in a medium bowl.

2. Dump the coated kale into your Air fryer basket. Set timer to cook at 370°F for about 4 to 5 minutes (do not preheat).

3. Shake the basket after 2 minutes. When the time is up.

4. Serve immediately and enjoy!

Ranch Seasoned Chickpeas

Preparation time: 5 minutes

Cooking time: 20 minutes

Overall time: 25 minutes

Serves: 3 to 4 people

Recipe Ingredients:

- 115 oz. can chickpeas (drained but not rinsed)
- 2 tbsp. of olive oil, divided
- 1 batch Homemade ranch seasoning
- 1 tsp. of sea salt
- 2 tbsp. of lemon juice

Cooking Instructions:

1. Toss the chickpeas and 1 tbsp. of the olive oil together. Then Air fry at 400°F for about 15 minutes.

2. After the 15 minutes, transfer the chickpeas back to your small bowl, and toss in the remaining oil, Ranch Seasoning, salt, and lemon juice to coat the beans.

3. Transfer the chickpeas back to the Air fryer basket, set timer to cook at 350°F for about 5 more minutes.

4. When the time is up, serve and enjoy!

Tortilla Chips

Preparation time: 2 minutes

Cooking time: 3 minutes

Overall time: 5 minutes

Recipe Ingredients:

- 8 corn tortillas
- 1 tablespoon of olive oil
- Salt to taste

Cooking Instructions:

1. Preheat Air fryer to 200°C. Use as sharp knife to cut corn tortillas into triangles.

2. Brush with olive oil. Place half of the tortilla pieces in wire basket. Set timer to Air fry for about 3 minutes.

3. Repeat with second batch. When the time is up.

4. Sprinkle with salt. Serve and enjoy!

CHAPTER 5: FISH & SEAFOODS

Fish and Chips

Overall time: 25 minutes

Serves: 3 to 4 people

Recipe Ingredients:

- 1 pack of fries (for four)
- 2 fish fillets
- 1 medium egg, beaten
- 3 slices of wholemeal bread, made into breadcrumbs
- 25g bag of tortilla chips
- 1 lemon (rind and juice)
- 1 tbsp. of parsley
- Salt and pepper to taste

Cooking Instructions:

1. Start by making the fries just like you would normally do. Then cut the fish fillets in half to make four nice sized pieces of fish for cooking.

2. Season the fish fillet with lemon juice and set aside. In a food processor, grind the breadcrumbs, lemon rind, parsley, tortillas and salt and pepper.

3. Place the breadcrumbs mixture it into a large baking tray. Cover the fish in the beaten egg and then in the breadcrumb's mixture.

4. Set your Air fryer to cook at 356°F (180°C) for about 15 minutes (until nice and crispy).

5. When the lovely fish smell fills your kitchen.

6. Serve immediately and enjoy!

Fish in Parchment paper

Preparation time: 10 minutes

Cooking time: 15 minutes

Overall time: 25 minutes

Serves: 2 people

Recipe Ingredients:

- 25-ounces cod fillets thawed
- ½ cup of julienned carrots
- ½ cup of julienned fennel bulbs or ¼ cup of julienned celery
- ½ cup of thinly sliced red peppers
- 2 sprigs tarragon or ½ tsp. of dried tarragon
- 2 pats melted butter
- 1 tbsp. of lemon juice
- 1 tbsp. of salt divided
- ½ tsp. of pepper
- 1 tbsp. of oil

Cooking Instructions:

1. Start by combining the melted butter, tarragon, ½ tsp. of salt, and lemon juice in a medium bowl.

2. Mix together until you get a creamy sauce. Then add the julienned vegetable and mix everything well. Reserve aside.

3. Cut two squares of parchment paper, large enough to hold your fish and vegetables.

4. Spray the fish fillets with oil evenly. Apply salt and pepper to both sides of the fish fillets. Lay one fish fillet down on each parchment square.

5. Top each fish fillet with half the vegetables and pour any remaining sauce over the vegetables.

6. Fold over the parchment paper, Crimp the sides to hold fish, ensure that veggies and sauce are securely inside the packet.

7. Place the packets inside your Air fryer basket. Set the Air fryer to cook at 350°F for about 15 minutes.

8. Carefully remove each packet to a plate and open just before serving.

9. Serve immediately and enjoy!

Lemon Garlic Shrimp

Preparation time: 5 minutes

Cooking time: 5 minutes

Overall time: 10 minutes

Serves: 3 to 4 people

Recipe Ingredients:

- 1 lb. of small shrimp (peeled with tails removed)
- 1 tbsp. of olive oil
- 4 garlic cloves, minced
- 1 lemon, zested and juiced
- 1 pinch crushed red pepper flakes (optional)
- ¼ cup of parsley, chopped
- ¼ tsp. of sea salt

Cooking Instructions:

1. Start by heating the Air fryer to 400°F. Combine the shrimp, olive oil, garlic, salt, lemon zest, and red pepper flakes in a medium mixing bowl.

2. Toss to coat thoroughly. Then transfer the shrimp to your Air fryer basket. Set your Air fryer to cook for about 5 to 8 minutes.

3. Shake the basket halfway through. When the time is up, pour the shrimp into a serving bowl and toss with lemon juice and parsley.

4. Season with additional salt to taste.

5. Serve immediately and enjoy!

Clean Eating Fish N' Chips

Preparation time: 15 minutes

Cooking time: 15 minutes

Overall time: 30 minutes

Serves: 3 to 4 people

Recipe Ingredients:

- 1¼ lb. of cod (We purchased it in small pieces instead of a fillet - either way works)
- 2 large eggs
- 1 cup of almond flour
- 1 tablespoon of dried parsley
- ½ teaspoon of garlic powder
- ½ teaspoon of onion powder
- ¼ teaspoon of salt
- 1 tablespoon of arrowroot powder OR organic corn starch

Cooking Instructions:

1. Beat the eggs with a whisk in a medium mixing bowl, until well combined.

2. In a separate bowl, mix together the almond flour, parsley, garlic powder, onion powder, salt and arrowroot powder (or corn starch if using).

3. Combine thoroughly. Dip the fish pieces into the egg, then roll in the breading, ensuring to cover each part of the fish.

4. Place the fish pieces in a single layer in your Air fryer basket. Set your Air fryer to cook at 350°F for about 7 minutes.

5. When the time is up, flip the pieces of fish in the basked and repeat for another 7 minutes.

6. When the time is up again, serve and enjoy!

Coconut Shrimp with Spicy Marmalade Sauce

Preparation time: 10 minutes

Cooking time: 20 minutes

Total time: 30 minutes

Serves: 2 to 3 people

Recipe Ingredients:

- 8 large shrimp shelled and deveined
- 8 oz. coconut milk
- ½ cup of shredded sweetened coconut
- ½ cup of panko bread
- ½ tsp. of Cayenner pepper
- ¼ tsp. of kosher salt
- ¼ tsp. of fresh ground pepper
- ½ cup of orange marmalade
- 1 tbsp. of honey
- 1 tsp. of mustard
- ¼ tsp. of hot sauce

Cooking Instructions:

1. Start by cleaning the shrimp and set aside. Whisk the coconut milk and season with salt and pepper in a small mixing bowl. Set aside.

2. Whisk together the coconut, panko, cayenne pepper, salt and pepper in a separate mixing bowl.

3. Dip the shrimp in the coconut milk, the panko (Do one at a time). Place them in your Air fryer basket.

4. Repeat the process until all the shrimp are coated thoroughly. Set your Air fryer to cook at 350°F for about 20 minutes (until the shrimp are cooked through).

5. While the shrimp are cooking, whisk together the marmalade, honey, mustard and hot sauce. Serve the shrimp with the sauce.

6. Serve immediately and enjoy!

Air fried Cajun Salmon

Serves: 1 to 2 people

Recipe Ingredients:

- 1 piece of fresh salmon fillet (about 200g)
- Cajun seasoning, enough to coat
- Sprinkle of sugar (optional)
- Juice from a quarter of lemon, to serve

Cooking Instructions:

1. Start by heating the Air fryer for 5 minutes. Clean your salmon and pat dry.

2. In a plate, sprinkle Cajun seasoning all over and make sure all sides are coated lightly.

3. If you prefer a tad of sweetness, add a light sprinkling of sugar. NO seasoning time required. We air fried direct.

4. For a salmon fillet about ¾ of an inch thick, Air fry for about 7 minutes, skin side up on the grill pan.

5. When the time is up, serve with a squeeze of lemon.

6. Serve immediately and enjoy!

Air Fried Crumbed Fish

Preparation time: 10 minutes

Cooking time: 12 minutes

Overall time: 22 minutes

Serves: 2 people

Recipe Ingredients:

- 4 tbsp. of vegetable oil
- 100g of breadcrumbs
- 1 egg, whisked
- 4 fish fillets
- 1 lemon, to serve

Cooking Instructions:

1. Preheat your air fryer to 180°C, mix together the oil and the breadcrumbs.

2. Continue stirring until the mixture becomes loose and crumbly. Dip the fillets into the egg.

3. shake off excess and dip the fillets into the crumb mixture. ensure it is evenly and fully covered.

4. Place the fillets in your Air fryer. Set to cook for about 12 minutes. (time varies depending on the thickness of the fish).

5. When the time is up, serve immediately with lemon and enjoy!

Coconut Shrimp and Apricot Sauce

Overall time: 35 minutes

Preparation time: 25 minutes

Cooking time: 10 minutes

Serves: 5 to 6 people

Recipe Ingredients:

- 1½ lb. of uncooked large shrimp
- 1½ cups of sweetened shredded coconut
- ½ cup of panko (Japanese) bread crumbs
- 4 large egg whites
- 3 dashes Louisiana-style hot sauce
- ¼ tsp. of salt
- ¼ tsp. of pepper
- ½ cup all-purpose flour

Sauce:

- 1 cup of apricot preserves
- 1 tsp. of cider vinegar
- ¼ tsp. of crushed red pepper flakes

Cooking Directions:

1. Preheat your air fryer to 375°F. Peel and devein shrimp, leaving tails on.

2. Toss coconut with bread crumbs in a shallow bowl. Whisk egg whites, hot sauce, salt and pepper in another shallow bowl.

3. In the third shallow bowl, Place flour. First dip shrimp in flour to coat lightly, shake off excess after dipping.

4. Dip in egg white mixture, then in coconut mixture, patting to help coating adhere.

5. Spray cooking spray on your Air fryer basket. Working in batches as needed.

6. Place the shrimp in a single layer in your Air fryer basket. Set to cook for about 4 minutes.

7. After the 4 minutes, turn shrimp and continue cooking until coconut is lightly browned and shrimp turn pink, (around 3 to 4 minutes).

8. In a saucepan, combine sauce ingredients, cook and stir over medium-low heat until preserves are melted.

9. Serve shrimp immediately with sauce.

10. Serve and enjoy!

Spicy Garlic Prawns

Preparation time: 12 minutes

Cooking time: 8 minutes

Overall time: 20 minutes

Serve: 3 people

Recipe Ingredients:

- 15 fresh prawns
- 1 ½ tbsp. of olive oil
- 1 tsp. of chili powder
- 1 tsp. of black pepper
- 1 tbsp. of sweet chili sauce
- 1 garlic, minced
- Salt

Cooking Directions:

1. Preheat your Air fryer at 180°C. Then wash and rinse the prawns in a clean water.

2. In a medium bowl, put the prawns and add the oil, chili powder, pepper, chili sauce and garlic.

3. Give everything a good stir and mix the ingredient so that the prawns are coated evenly.

4. Add salt and pepper to taste. Place the prawns into the Air fryer at 180°C.

5. Set your Air fryer to cook the prawns for about 8 minutes.

6. Serve and enjoy!

Fried Cod Fish

Overall time: 15 to 20 minutes

Serves: 3 to 4 people

Recipe Ingredients:

- 2 x 7 oz. (200g) cod fish
- Sprinkle of salt and sugar
- A dash of sesame oil
- 1 cup (250ml) of water
- 5 tbsp. of light soy sauce
- 1 tsp. of dark soy sauce
- 5 little cubes of rock sugar
- 3 tbsp. of oil
- 5 slices of ginger
- 4 one-inch white parts of spring onion
- 1 handful green part of spring onions to garnish, shredded
- Corriander to garnish (a handful)

Cooking Instructions:

1. Start by washing cod fish, after washing pat dry cod fish. Season cod fish with salt and sugar plus a dash of sesame oil.

2. keep the cod fish aside for about 15 minutes. Then preheat the Air fryer for 3 minutes at 356°F (180°C).

3. Do not add oil, fish has natural oils. Air fry cod fish for about 12 minutes (until skin is crispy).

4. In the meantime, prepare the seasoning sauce. Pour water into a pan and bring to boil.

5. Then, add light soy sauce, dark soy sauce and rock sugar, give everything a good stir until sugar melts.

6. Heat up the oil in a small pan and add ginger and white part of spring onion.

7. Fry until the ginger turns brown. After frying the ginger, remove the ginger and spring onion sections.

8. Place the code fish in a dish. Top with garnish. Pour the boiling oil over the fish.

9. Spoon seasoning sauce over the serve immediately.

Southern Style Catfish with Green Beans

Overall time: 25 minutes

Serves: 2 (serving size: 1 fillet, 1 cup green beans, 1 tbsp. sauce)

Recipe Ingredients:

- 12 oz. fresh green beans, trimmed
- Cooking spray
- 1 tsp. of light brown sugar
- ½ tsp. of crushed red pepper (optional)
- 3/8 tsp. of kosher salt, divided
- 2 Unit (6-oz.) catfish fillets
- ¼ cup all-purpose flour
- 1 large egg, lightly beaten
- 1/3 cup of panko (Japanese-style breadcrumbs)
- ¼ tsp. of black pepper
- 2 tbsp. of mayonnaise
- 1½ tsp. of finely chopped fresh dill
- ¾ tsp. of dill pickle relish
- ½ tsp. of apple cider vinegar
- 1/8 tsp. of granulated sugar
- Lemon wedges

Cooking Instructions:

1. Start by placing green beans in a medium bowl, spray liberally with cooking spray.

2. Sprinkle with brown sugar, crushed red pepper (if using), and 1/8 tsp. of the salt.

3. Place them in the basket of your Air fryer. Set to cook at 400°F for about 12 minutes (until well browned and tender).

4. When the time is up, transfer to a bowl and cover with aluminum foil to keep warm.

5. Toss the catfish in flour to coat, after coating thoroughly shake off excess. Dip pieces, 1 at a time, in egg to coat.

6. Sprinkle with panko, pressing to coat evenly on all sides. Then place the fish in your Air fryer basket and spray with cooking spray.

7. Set your Air fryer to cook at 400°F for about 8 minutes (until browned and cooked through).

8. When the time is up, sprinkle tops evenly with pepper and remaining ¼ tsp. of salt.

9. While fish is cooking, whisk mayonnaise, dill, relish, vinegar, and sugar together in a small mixing bowl.

10. Serve fish and green beans with tartar sauce and lemon wedges.

11. Serve and enjoy!

Salmon Fishcakes Crumb

Overall time: 1 hr 15 minutes

Serves: 3 to 4 people

Recipe Ingredients:

- 9 ounces (250g) salmon, cooked
- 14 ounces (400g) potato, cold mashed
- 1 small handful capers
- 1 small handful parsley, chopped
- Zest of 1 lemon
- 2 ounces (50g) plain flour, for coating
- Spray oil

Cooking Instructions:

1. Flake the salmon. Combine with the mashed potato, capers, dill and zest. Season well.

2. Shape into small cakes and dust with flour. Chill in the fridge for 1 hour to firm up.

3. Preheat your Air fryer to 356°F (180°C). Then place the fishcakes in the basket of your Air fryer.

4. Spray with oil, set your Air fryer to cook for about 7 minutes (until golden).

5. When the time is up, serve and enjoy!

Fish Paste Fritter

Total time: 20 mins

Serves: 5 to 6 people

Recipe Ingredients:

- 3 pairs of dried dough fritter (You Tiao)
- 200g of fish paste
- 1 tsp. of sesame oil
- 1 tsp. of sugar
- 1 tsp. of ground white pepper
- 20 grams of carrot, chopped
- 20 grams of spring onion, finely chopped
- 75g of prawn, finely chopped
- 2 egg whites
- 3 tbsp. of corn flour
- Olive oil
- Sesame seeds (For Garnish)

Cooking Directions:

1. First, split the dough fritter apart and cut them into 5 to 2-inch pieces. Cut a slit in the middle soft part of fritter to make a hole.

2. In a medium bowl, add the fish paste, sesame oil, sugar, pepper, sugar, onion, prawn, egg whites and corn flour.

3. Give everything a good mix to combine well. Carefully spread the paste into each dough fritter.

4. Preheat your Air Fryer at 160°C and set the Air fryer to cook for about 3 minutes. Generously coat the Air Fryer basket with oil.

5. Place the fritter into your Air fryer basket. Set your Air fryer to cook the fritter for about 10 minutes.

6. When the time is up, serve and enjoy.

CHAPTER 6: POULTRY RECIPES

Artichoke Chicken

Overall time: 1 hr. 5 minutes

Preparation time: 15 minutes

Bake time: 50 minutes

Serves: 7 to 8 people

Recipe Ingredients:

- 8 boneless skinless chicken breast halves (4 oz. each)
- 2 tbsp. of butter
- 2 jars (6 oz. each) marinated quartered artichoke hearts, drained
- 1 jar (4½ oz.) whole mushrooms, drained
- ½ cup of chopped onion
- 1/3 cup all-purpose flour
- 1½ tsp. of dried rosemary, crushed
- ¾ tsp. of salt
- ¼ tsp. of pepper
- 2 cups of chicken broth or (1 cup of broth and 1 cup of dry white wine)
- Hot cooked noodles
- Fresh parsley, minced

Cooking Instructions:

1. In a large skillet, brown the chicken in butter. After browning chicken, remove chicken to an ungreased 13x9-in. baking dish.

2. Then arrange artichokes and mushrooms on top of chicken and set aside. Sauté the onion in pan juices (until crisp-tender).

3. In a medium mixing bowl, combine the flour, rosemary, salt and pepper. Stir into pan until blended.

4. Add in the chicken broth and bring to a boil, cook and stir constantly until thickened and bubbly, for about 1 to 2 minutes.

5. Remove from the heat, spoon over chicken and Bake uncovered at 350° until a thermometer inserted in the chicken reads 170°, for about 35 to 40 minutes.

6. Serve with pasta and sprinkle with parsley. Serve and enjoy!

Quentin's Peach-Bourbon Wings

Overall time: 50 minutes

Preparation time: 35 minutes

Cooking time: 15 minutes

Makes about 1½ dozen pieces

Recipe Ingredients:

- ½ cup of peach preserves
- 1 tbsp. of brown sugar
- 1 garlic clove, minced
- ¼ tsp. of salt
- 2 tbsp. of white vinegar
- 2 tbsp. of bourbon
- 1 tsp. of corn starch
- 1½ tsp. of water
- 2 lb. of chicken wings

Cooking Instructions:

1. Start by heating your Air fryer to 400°F. Place the preserves, brown sugar, garlic and salt in a food processor, process until blended.

2. After blending the mixture, transfer to a small saucepan. Add vinegar and bourbon, bring to a boil.

3. Reduce heat, simmer, uncovered, until slightly thickened, for about 4 to 6 minutes.

4. Mix cornstarch and water in a small mixing bowl, until smooth. Stir into preserve mixture.

5. Return to a boil. Cook and stir constantly for about 1 to 2 minutes (until thickened).

6. Reserve ¼ cup of sauce for serving. Use a sharp knife, cut through the two joints on each chicken wing.

7. Discard wing tips. Spray the basket of your Air fryer with cooking oil. (Work in batches as needed).

8. Place chicken wing pieces in a single layer in the basket of your Air fryer. Set your Air fryer to cook for about 6 minutes.

9. After the 6 minutes, turn and brush with preserve mixture. Return to your Air fryer, cook until browned and juices run clear, for about 6 to 8 minutes longer.

10. Remove and keep warm. Repeat with remaining wing pieces.

11. Serve wings immediately with reserved sauce.

12. Serve and enjoy!

Chicken Breast

Recipe Ingredients:

- 5 to 6 oz. chicken breasts split in half lengthwise
- Seasoning salt of choice
- Salt and pepper to taste

Cooking Instructions:

1. Set the Air fryer to 400°F. Slice the chicken breast in half and season with salt and pepper.

2. Place the chicken in the basket of your Air fryer, set the temperature to 400°F.

3. Close the basket and set the timer to cook for about 7 minutes. When the time is up.

4. Take the chicken out and flip, cook for another 4 minutes longer.

5. After the 4 minutes, remove and serve.

6. Serve immediately and enjoy.

Sizzling Turkey Fajitas Platter

Preparation time: 5 minutes

Cooking time: 20 minutes

Overall time: 25 minutes

Serves: 2 people

Recipe Ingredients:

- 6 tortilla wraps
- 100 g leftover turkey breast
- 1 large avocado
- 1 large yellow pepper
- 1 large red pepper
- 1 large green pepper
- ½ small red onion
- 5 tablespoons of soft cheese
- 3 tablespoons of Cajun spice
- 2 tablespoons of Mexican seasoning
- 1 teaspoon of cumin
- Salt & pepper
- Fresh coriander

Cooking Instructions:

1. Slice up the salad. Chop your avocado into little wedges and dice the red onion.

2. Slice the peppers into thin slices and chop up the turkey breast into small little chunks.

3. After chopping the turkey breast, place the turkey, peppers and onions into a bowl.

4. Mix with all the seasonings along with the soft cheese. Place in silver foil and Air fry for about 20 minutes on 200°C.

5. When the time is up, serve and enjoy!

Rotisserie Style Whole Chicken

Preparation time: 5 minutes

Cooking time: 1 hour

Overall time: 1 hour 5 minutes

Serves: 3 to 4 people

Recipe Ingredients:

- 1 whole chicken cleaned and blotted dry
- 2 tbsp. of Ghee (or coconut or olive oil)
- 1 tbsp. of TOG house seasoning

Cooking Instructions:

1. Remove giblet packet from chicken and pat dry. Rub Ghee/Oil all over the chicken. Season generously with TOG house seasoning.

2. Place the chicken breast side down into your Air fryer. Set timer to cook at 350°F for about 30 minutes.

3. After the 30 minutes, flip chicken over and cook at 350°F for an additional 30 minutes.

4. When the time is up, let rest for about 10 minutes.

5. Serve immediately and enjoy!

Greek Stuffed Chicken Breast

Preparation time: 10 minutes

Cooking time: 15 minutes

Overall time: 25 minutes

Serves: 3 to 4 people

Recipe Ingredients:

- 26-oz. boneless skinless chicken breasts
- 1 cup of wild rice, prepared
- 4 oz. fat-free feta cheese
- 4 tbsp. of `Greek salad dressing

Cooking Instructions:

1. Start by slicing the chicken breasts in half, making a total of 4 pieces of chicken.

2. Between two pieces of parchment paper, pound the chicken breasts until thin.

3. Mix prepared wild rice, 1 tbsp. of Greek dressing, and fat-free feta cheese together in a medium mixing bowl.

4. Place ¼ rice mixture onto center of each chicken breast and roll covering mixture.

5. Place each chicken breasts rolled side down into your Air fryer pan. Brush the remaining Greek dressing over the tops of your chicken breasts.

6. Set timer to cook at 382°F for about 15 minutes. When the time is up.

7. Serve immediately and enjoy!

Air Fried Buffalo Chicken Strips

Serves: 2 to 3 people

Recipe Ingredients:

- 12 ounces chicken breast strips
- ¾ cup of Panko crumbs or bread crumbs
- ¼ cup of flour (We use gluten free flour from Trader Joes)
- 1 egg (or liquid egg whites)
- Buffalo Sauce - (We used about 1/2 cup)
- Garlic salt and pepper to taste

Cooking Instructions:

1. In a separate bowl, place egg, flour and panko crumbs. (We mixed the panko with some garlic salt & pepper).

2. Spray a little cooking spray on the bottom of your Air fryer. Dip chicken in the flour, then the egg, then the panko until well coated.

3. Place the chicken in your Air fryer, spray the top of the chicken with a little more cooking spray.

4. Set the timer to fry at 375°F for about 10 minutes. After the 10 minutes, flip and cook for an additional 3 to 5 minutes.

5. When the time is up, remove chicken from your Air fryer. Place in a mixing bowl and toss in buffalo sauce until well coated.

6. Serve with celery, carrots and ranch.

7. Serve and enjoy!

Whole30 Lemon Pepper Chicken

Preparation time: 3 minutes

Cooking time: 15 minutes

Total time: 18 minutes

Serves: 1

Recipe Ingredients:

- 1 chicken breast
- 2 lemons rind and juice
- 1 tablespoon of chicken seasoning
- 1 teaspoon of garlic puree
- Handful black peppercorns
- Salt & pepper

Cooking Instructions:

1. Start by heating your Air fryer to 180°C. Set up your work station. Place a large sheet of silver foil on the work top.

2. Add all the seasonings to it and the lemon rind. Lay out the chicken breasts onto a chopping board.

3. Trim off any fatty bits and any little bones. Season each side with salt and pepper.

4. Rub the chicken seasoning into both sides of the chicken breast so that it is slightly a different color.

5. Place it in the silver foil sheet, rub it thoroughly so that it is fully seasoned. Seal it up very tight so that it can't breathe.

6. Give it a slap with a rolling pin so that it will flatten it out and release more flavor.

7. Place it in your Air fryer. Set your Air fryer to cook for about 15 minutes. After the 15 minutes, check to see if it is fully cooked in the middle before serving.

8. Serve immediately and enjoy!

Popcorn Chicken

Preparation time: 10 minutes

Cooking time: 10 minutes

Overall time: 20 minutes

Serves: 2 to 3 people

Recipe Ingredients:

- 1 lb. of skinless chicken tenders (cut into small cubes)
- ½ cup of corn starch
- 1 cup of unsweetened lite culinary coconut milk
- 1 teaspoon of pickle juice
- 3 cups of finely crushed gluten-free corn flake cereal
- ½ teaspoon of garlic powder
- ½ teaspoon of onion powder
- ½ teaspoon of paprika
- ¼ teaspoon of black pepper
- ¼ teaspoon of cayenne pepper (optional)

Cooking Instructions:

1. After cutting the chicken tenders into small cube, place them to the side. Set up your 3 coating stations, in order.

2. First, make a plate of the corn starch. In the second bowl, mix together the coconut milk and pickle juice.

3. In a plastic bag, crush the corn flakes with the spices before pouring out onto a plate.

4. After setting up 3 coating station, take each chicken piece, coat in the corn starch, then dunk in the coconut milk, and finally roll in the corn flake crumbs.

5. Place the coated chicken piece in the basket of your Air fryer. Repeat for all the pieces of chicken, evenly spacing them out in the Air fryer basket.

6. You can make two batches depending on the size of your Air fryer. Set the Air fryer to 400°F and the time to 10 minutes (7-8 minutes if doing two batches).

7. Now let it cook and get your ketchup ready to enjoy.

8. Serve and enjoy!

Tandoori Chicken

Preparation time: 15 minutes

Cooking time: 30 minutes

Overall time: 45 minutes

Serves: 3 to 4 people

Recipe Ingredients:

- Chicken leg With Thigh - 4

For the first Marinade

- 3 teaspoons of ginger paste
- 3 teaspoons of garlic paste
- Salt to taste
- 3 tbsp. of lemon juice

For the second Marinade

- 2 tablespoons of tandoori masala powder
- 1 teaspoon of roasted cumin powder
- 1 teaspoon of garam masala powder
- 2 teaspoons of red chili powder
- 1 teaspoon of turmeric powder
- 4 tbsp. of hung curd
- A pinch of orange food colour (Optional)
- 2 teaspoons of Kasuri Methi
- 1 teaspoon of black pepper powder
- 2 teaspoon of coriander powder

Cooking Instructions:

1. Wash the chicken legs, use a knife to make slits in them. In a large bowl, add the chicken with the ingredients for the first marinade.

2. Mix well and set aside for about 15 minutes. Mix the ingredients for the second marinade together.

3. Pour them over the chicken and mix well. Cover the bowl and refrigerate for up to 10 to 12 hours.

4. Line the basket of your Air fryer with aluminum foil. preheat to 230°C. Place the chicken on the Air fryer basket.

5. Air fry for about 18 to 20 minutes, until slightly charred and browned.

6. Serve hot with Yogurt mint dip and Onion rings. Serve and enjoy!

Rotisserie Chicken

Serves: 3 to 4 people

Recipe Ingredients:

- 1 whole chicken
- 1 tablespoon of avocado oil
- 2 tbsp. of primal palate super gyro seasoning
- 2 tablespoons of primal palate new bae seasoning
- 1 tablespoon of Himalayan pink salt

Cooking Instructions:

1. Start by heating your Air fryer to 375°F. wash the chicken with clean water and Pat the chicken dry.

2. Drizzle with avocado oil. Season with half the seasonings. Place the whole chicken in the basket of your Air fryer.

3. Set timer to cook for about 30 minutes. After the 30 minutes, open the Air fryer. Flip the chicken and add the remaining seasoning.

4. After flipping the chicken, set timer to cook the chicken for another 30 minutes.

5. Once the chicken is done cooking, remove the chicken from the basket.

6. Allow it to cool for about 5 minutes before slicing and serving.

7. Serve and enjoy!

Garlic Parmesan Chicken Tenders

Preparation time: 5 minutes

Cooking time: 12 minutes

Serves: 3 to 4 people

Recipe Ingredients:

- 8 chicken tenders, raw
- 1 egg
- 2 tbsp. of water
- Canola or non-fat cooking spray

For the dredge coating:

- 1 cup of panko breadcrumbs
- ½ teaspoon of salt
- ¼ teaspoon of ground black pepper
- 1 teaspoons of garlic powder
- ½ teaspoon of onion powder
- ¼ cup of parmesan cheese
- Serve with homemade ranch dressing.

Cooking Instructions:

1. In a big mixing bowl, combine the dredge coating ingredients. (Use a bowl big enough to fit the chicken pieces.

2. Place egg and water to the second bowl, make sure it is large enough for dredging.

3. Whisk to combine. Then dip the chicken tenders into the egg wash and then into the panko dredge mixture.

4. Place the breaded tenders into the basket of your Air fryer. Repeat with remaining tenders.

5. Place the Fry Basket into the Air fryer and spray a light coat of canola oil of non-fat cooking spray over the panko.

6. Set your Air fryer to 400°F and cook for about 12 minutes. Halfway through cooking, flip the tenders over.

7. Serve and enjoy!

Huli Huli Chicken

Preparation time: 40 minutes

Cooking time: 10 minutes

Total time: 50 minutes

Serves: 3 to 4 people

Recipe Ingredients:

- 4 boneless, skinless chicken thighs, about 1.5 pounds
- **For the Sauce:**
- 8 oz. of canned pineapple chunks
- ¼ cup of soy sauce
- ¼ cup of sugar
- 2 tablespoons of ketchup
- 1 tbsp. garlic, minced
- 1 tablespoon of ginger, minced
- ¼ cup of green onion, chopped

Cooking Instructions:

1. Pork holes into the chicken with fork and place the chicken in a large bowl or in a Ziploc bag.

2. Prepare the sauce with the sauce ingredients. Take ¼ cup of juice from the canned pineapple and set aside the pineapple chunks.

3. In a small microwave safe bowl, mix together the ¼ cup of pineapple juice, soy sauce, sugar, ketchup, ginger and garlic.

4. Pour half of the sauce over the chicken and mix it with the chicken until the thighs are well-coated with the marinade.

5. Reserve the remaining sauce to cook as your dipping sauce. Set the chicken aside to marinade for about 30 minutes or up to 24 hours in the refrigerator.

6. Place the marinated chicken in your Air Fryer basket. Set your Air fryer at 360°F.

7. Cook the chicken for about 15 minutes, turning half way through. In a microwave, place the reserved sauce.

8. Cook the reserved sauce on high for about 45 to 60 seconds, stirring every 15 seconds.

9. Cook the sauce until you get a thick glaze or pouring sauce that can be used with the cooked chicken

10. Using a meat thermometer, ensure that the chicken has reached an internal temperature of 165°F.

11. Remove the chicken from the Air Fryer and place on a serving tray. Garnish the chicken with pineapples and green onions.

12. Serve with the thickened sauce poured over all of it.

13. Serve and enjoy!

Chicken Cordon Bleu

Preparation time: 10 minutes

Cooking time: 30 minutes

Overall time: 40 minutes

Recipe Ingredients:

- 2 chicken breasts
- 1 tbsp. of thyme
- 1 tbsp. of tarragon
- 1 teaspoon of Parsley
- 1 tsp. of garlic puree
- 1 egg
- 20 grams of oats
- 1 slice ham
- 1 tbsp. of soft cheese
- 1 slice cheddar cheese
- A pinch of salt
- Freshly ground pepper to taste

Cooking Instructions:

1. Start by preheating your Air fryer to 360°F.

2. Cut the chicken at an angle to right near to the corner to enable you fold them over.

3. Add the ingredients to the center and sprinkle the tarragon, salt and pepper, lightly covering the chicken.

4. In a small mixing bowl, mix together the soft cheese, garlic and parsley. Spread a layer of the soft cheese mixture in the middle of the chicken.

5. Add half a slice of both the cheddar cheese and ham. Place the chicken and seal it with the filling. In a separate bowl, beat the egg.

6. In another bowl, blend the oats, and mix it with the thyme. Roll the chicken in the oats, the egg and back in the oats.

7. Place the chicken pieces into your Air fryer. Set your Air fryer to cook for about 30 minutes at 360°F, turning half way through.

8. After the 30 minutes. Serve and enjoy!

Pizza Stuffed Chicken

Preparation time: 10 minutes

Cooking time: 15 minutes

overall time: 25 minutes

Serves: 2 to 3 people

Recipe Ingredients:

- 5 boneless skinless, chicken thighs
- ½ cup of pizza sauce
- 14 slices of turkey pepperoni
- ½ small red onion sliced
- 5 ounce of sliced mozzarella cheese
- ½ cup of shredded cheese for topping

Cooking Instructions:

1. Open the chicken thighs and lay them flat on a piece of parchment paper.

2. Place the second piece of parchment paper over the chicken. Pound the chicken to create a thin piece.

3. Spoon on a tbsp. of pizza sauce on each piece of the chicken and spread it evenly. Place 3 pieces of turkey pepperoni on top of the sauce.

4. Add one slice of Mozzarella cheese. Fold one side of the chicken over on to the other. Use a toothpick to hold the chicken together.

5. Once cooked it stays together on its own. Preheat your Air fryer to 370°F for about 2 minutes.

6. Grease the tray, and lay the pieces out in a single layer. Add the chicken and set you Air fryer to cook for about 6 minutes.

7. After the 6 minutes, Flip the chicken and cook for another 6 minutes. For the last 3 minutes, add cheese to melt on the top.

8. Cooking time may vary depending on how thick your chicken pieces are. Always check chicken thighs to ensure they are heated to 165F.

9. When the time is up, serve and enjoy!

Turkish Chicken Kabab Tavuk Shish

Preparation time: 45 minutes

Cooking time: 10 minutes

Total time: 55 minutes

Serves: 3 to 4 people

Recipe Ingredients:

- ¼ cup of plain Greek yogurt
- 1 tablespoon of minced garlic
- 1 tablespoon of tomato paste
- 1 tbsp. of vegetable oil
- 1 tablespoon of lemon juice
- 1 teaspoon of salt
- 1 tsp. of ground cumin
- 1 teaspoon of paprika
- ½ teaspoon of ground cinnamon
- ½ teaspoon of black pepper
- ½ teaspoon of cayenne pepper
- 1 pound of boneless, skinless, chicken thighs, each cut into 4 pieces

Cooking Instructions:

1. In a medium bowl, stir together the Greek yogurt, garlic, tomato paste, lemon juice, oil, and salt.

2. Then stir in the cumin, paprika, cinnamon, black pepper, and cayenne pepper until the spices are well-blended into the yogurt.

3. Add the chicken pieces and mix everything thoroughly until the chicken is has evenly coated with the marinade.

4. Let the chicken to marinate for about 30 minutes. Remove the chicken from the marinade and arrange in a single layer in your Air fryer basket.

5. Set your Air fryer to cook the chicken at 370°F for about 10 minutes. Flip the chicken halfway to brown the chicken evenly.

6. Set the Air Fryer to 370°F and cook the chicken for additional 5 minutes. After the additional 5 minutes, test the chicken with a thermometer.

7. Make use of a meat thermometer to test the chicken to ensure that the chicken has reached an internal temperature of 150°F before serving.

8. Serve and enjoy.

Zinger Chicken Burger

Preparation time: 10 minutes

Cooking time: 15 minutes

Overall time: 25 minutes

Serves: 3 to 4 people

Recipe Ingredients:

- 6 chicken breasts
- 1 small egg beaten
- 50g plain flour
- 10 ml KFC spice blend
- 100 ml bread crumbs
- 1 teaspoon of Worcester sauce
- 1 teaspoon of mustard powder
- 1 teaspoon of paprika
- Salt & pepper

Cooking Instructions:

1. Mince the chicken in the food processor. Add the Worcester sauce, mustard, paprika and salt and pepper in the food processor.

2. Make the chicken into burger shapes, put them to one side. Add the egg in one bowl. In another bowl add the flour.

3. In the third bowl, add your KFC spice blend, mix with your bread crumbs. Cover your Zinger burgers in the flour, the egg and then the bread crumbs.

4. Place them in your Air fryer. Set your Air fryer to 180°C for about 15 minutes or until the chicken is cooked in the Centre.

5. When the time is up, serve and enjoy!

Thai Peanut Chicken Egg Rolls

Preparation time: 10 minutes

Cooking time: 8 minutes

Overall time: 18 minutes

Serves: 3 to 4 people

Recipe Ingredients:

- 4 egg roll wrappers
- 2 cups of rotisserie chicken shredded
- ¼ cup of Thai peanut sauce
- 1 medium carrot very thinly sliced
- 3 green onions, chopped
- ¼ red bell pepper julienned
- Non-stick cooking spray or sesame oil

Cooking Instructions:

1. Preheat your Air fryer to 390°F. Toss the chicken with the Thai peanut sauce in a small mixing bowl.

2. On a clean dry surface, lay the egg roll wrappers out. Over the bottom third of an egg roll wrapper, arrange ¼ the carrot, bell pepper and onions.

3. Spoon ½ cup of the chicken mixture over the vegetables. Moisten the outside edges of the wrapper with water.

4. Fold the sides of the wrapper toward the center, roll tightly. Repeat with remaining wrappers.

5. Keep remaining wrappers covered with a damp paper towel until ready to use. Spray the cooking spray to the assembled egg rolls.

6. Turn the egg rolls over and spray the back sides also. Place the egg rolls in your Air fryer.

7. Bake at 390° for about 6 to 8 minutes or until they are crispy and golden brown.

8. When the time is up, slice in half and serve with additional Thai Peanut Sauce for dipping.

9. Serve immediately and enjoy!

Chicken Drumsticks

Preparation time: 3 minutes

Cooking time: 17 minutes

Overall time: 20 minutes

Recipe Ingredients:

- 1 tsp. of salt
- 1 tsp. of black pepper
- 2 tbsp. of house Montreal chicken seasoning
- 600 grams of chicken drumsticks
- Oil

Cooking Instructions:

1. Start by preheating your Air fryer to 390°F.

2. Generously rub the oil all over the chicken and season both sides of the chicken with the seasoning mix.

3. Place the seasoned chicken into the Air fryer basket. Set your Air fryer to air-fry for about 10 minutes.

4. Turn the chicken halfway through to brown evenly. Lower the heat to 300°F and cook for additional 6 minutes.

5. When the time is up, remove the chicken from your Air fryer, allow the chicken to rest for about 2 minutes before serving.

6. Serve and enjoy!

CHAPTER 7: MEAT RECIPES

Stromboli

Serves: 3 to 4 people

Recipe Ingredients:

- 12 oz. of pizza crust, refrigerated
- 3 cups of cheddar cheese, shredded
- 0.75 cup of Mozzarella cheese, shredded
- 0.333333 lb. of cooked ham, sliced
- 3 oz. of red bell peppers, roasted
- 1 egg yolk
- 1 tbsp. of milk

Cooking Instructions:

1. Roll the dough out until ¼ inch thick. Layer the ham, cheese and peppers on one side of the dough and fold over to seal.

2. Mix the egg and milk together, brush the dough. Place the Stromboli into the basket of your Air fryer.

3. Place it into the Air fryer. Set your Air fryer to 360°F and cook for about 15 minutes.

4. Flip the Stromboli over every 5 minutes.

5. When the time is up, serve and enjoy!

BBQ pork ribs

Overall time: 35 minutes

Serve: 2 people

Recipe Ingredients:

- 500g of pork ribs
- 3 cloves of garlic, chopped
- 4 tbsp. of BBQ sauce
- 1 tbsp. of honey
- ½ tsp. of five spices powder
- 1 tsp. of sesame oil
- 1 tsp. of salt
- 1 tsp. of black pepper
- 1 tsp. of soy sauce

Cooking Instructions:

1. Start by washing the pork ribs, chop pork ribs into small pieces. Place the pork ribs into a mixing bowl.

2. In a mixing bowl, add garlic, BBQ sauce, honey, five spices powder, sesame oil, salt, pepper and soy sauce.

3. Marinate well. Keep in fridge for up to 4 hours. Preheat your Air fryer for about 5 minutes at 180°C.

4. Place the pork ribs into your Air fryer. Set timer to cook for about 15 minutes.

5. Lightly coat the pork ribs with honey. After the 15 minutes, turn the pork ribs and cook for another 15 minutes.

6. When the time is up, Serve and enjoy!

Memphis-Style BBQ Pork Ribs

Serves: 2 people

Recipe Ingredients:

- 1 tbsp. of kosher salt
- 1 tbsp. of dark brown sugar
- 1 tbsp. of sweet paprika
- 1 tsp. of garlic powder
- 1 tsp. of onion powder
- 1 tsp. of poultry seasoning
- ½ tsp. of mustard powder
- ½ tsp. of freshly ground black pepper
- 2¼ lb. of individually cut St. Louis–style pork spareribs

Cooking Instructions:

1. Whisk the salt, brown sugar, paprika, garlic powder, onion powder, poultry seasoning, mustard powder, and pepper together in a large mixing bowl.

2. Add the ribs in the large bowl with mixture, toss and coat the ribs with the seasonings.

3. Arrange the ribs in the basket of your Air fryer. Arrange them standing up on their ends and leaned up against the wall of the basket and each other.

4. Set your Air fryer to cook at 350°F until the ribs are tender inside and golden brown and crisp on the outside, for about 35 minutes.

5. When the time is up, transfer the ribs to plates and serve hot.

6. Serve and enjoy!

Mongolian Beef

Preparation time: 20 minutes

Cooking time: 20 minutes

Overall time: 40 minutes

Serves: 3 to 4 people

Recipe Ingredients:

For the meat:

- 1 lb. of flank steak
- ¼ cup of corn starch

For the sauce:

- 2 teaspoons of vegetable oil
- ½ teaspoon of ginger
- 1 tablespoon of minced garlic
- ½ cup of soy sauce or gluten free soy sauce
- ½ cup of water
- ¾ cup of brown sugar packed

Extras:

- Cooked rice
- Green beans
- Green onions

Cooking Instructions:

1. Thinly slice the steak in long pieces, coat with the corn starch. Place them in your Air fryer.

2. Set your Air fryer to cook on 390°F for about 10 minutes on each side. While the steak cooks.

3. In a medium sized saucepan, warm up all sauce ingredient on medium-high heat.

4. Then whisk the ingredients together until it gets to a low boil. Once both the steak and sauce are cooked.

5. Place the steak in a bowl with the sauce and let it soak in for 5 to 10 minutes. When ready to serve.

6. Use tongs to remove the steak and let the excess sauce drip off. Place steak on cooked rice and green beans.

7. Top with additional sauce if you desire.

8. Serve immediately and enjoy!

Beef Empanadas

Overall time: 26 minutes

Preparation time: 10 minutes

Cooking time: 16 minutes

Recipe Ingredients:

- 8 Goya empanada discs (in frozen section), thawed
- 1 cup of picadillo
- 1 egg white, whisked
- 1 tsp. of water

Cooking Instructions:

1. Preheat your Air fryer to 325°F for about 8 minutes. Spray the basket generously with cooking spray.

2. Place 2 tablespoons of picadillo in the center of each disc. Fold in half and use a fork to seal the edges.

3. Repeat with the remaining dough. Whisk the egg whites with water and brush the tops of the empanadas.

4. Bake 2 at a time in your Air fryer for about 8 minutes, or until golden. After the 8 minutes.

5. Remove from heat and repeat with the remaining empanadas.

6. Serve and enjoy!

Steak with Roasted Potatoes

Overall time: 30 minutes

Serves: 1

Recipe Ingredients:

- 4 small potatoes, chopped
- 1 tbsp. of olive oil
- 1 tsp. of cayenne pepper
- 1 tsp. of Italian herbs
- 1 tsp. of salt
- 200g (70 oz.) striploin steak
- ½ tbsp. of olive oil
- Salt and pepper to taste

Cooking Instructions:

1. Start by adding potatoes, olive oil, cayenne pepper, Italian herbs and salt in a medium mixing bowl. Mix evenly.

2. Preheat your Air fryer to 180°C (356°F) for about 5 minutes. Place the potatoes into the basket of your Air fryer.

3. Set your Air fryer to cook for about 16 minutes. Toss the potatoes half way. When the time is up, set aside.

4. Rub oil, salt and pepper on both side of the steak. Place the steak into your Air fryer and cook at 200°C (392°F) for about 7 to 13 minutes.

5. Depending on preference of steak doneness. Serve with the roasted potatoes.

6. Serve and enjoy!

Vietnamese Grilled Pork Thit Nuong

Preparation time: 40 minutes

Cooking time: 10 minutes

Overall time: 50 minutes

Serves: 3 to 4 people

Recipe Ingredients:

For the Marinade:

- ¼ cup of minced onions
- 2 tbsp. of oil
- 1 tbsp. of Splenda or 2 tbsp. of sugar
- 2 tsp. of dark soy sauce
- 1 tbsp. of minced garlic
- 1 tbsp. of fish sauce
- 1 tbsp. of minced lemongrass paste
- ½ tsp. of pepper
- 1 lb. of thinly sliced pork shoulder

For Finishing:

- ¼ cup of crushed roasted peanuts
- 2 tablespoons of cilantro, chopped

Cooking Directions:

1. In a medium bowl, whisk together the onions, sugar, soy sauce, oil, garlic, fish sauce, lemongrass, and pepper.

2. Slice the pork shoulder into ½ in slices and use a knife to cut the crossways into 4-inch pieces.

3. Add the pork to the marinade and allow it to rest for about 30 minutes or refrigerate in the fridge for up to 24 hours.

4. Remove the pork slices from the marinade, and place in single layer in your Air fryer basket.

5. Air fryer to 400°F and cook the pork for about 10 minutes, flipping over halfway to brown evenly. Then test the pork with meat thermometer.

6. Use a meat thermometer to test the pork and ensure that the pork has reached an internal temperature of 165°F.

7. Remove the pork from the Air fryer and place to a serving tray.

8. Sprinkle the pork with the roasted peanuts and cilantro.

9. Serve and enjoy!

Steak

Recipe Ingredients:

1 New York strip steak (We used almost a pound)

Cooking Instructions:

1. Preheat your Air fryer to 400°F for about 5 minutes.

2. Then place the steak in the Air fryer, season it with seasoning of choice.

3. Set the timer to cook for about 12 minutes. Flip the steak at 6 minutes.

4. Serve with vegetables or mashed cauliflower.

5. Serve and enjoy!

Crispy Breaded Pork Chops

Overall time: 15 minutes

Recipe Ingredients:

- Olive oil spray
- 6 (¾-inch thick) centre cut boneless pork chops, fat trimmed (5 oz. each)
- Kosher salt
- 1 large egg, beaten
- ½ cup of panko crumbs (check labels for GF)
- 1/3 cup of crushed cornflakes crumbs
- 2 tablespoons of grated parmesan cheese
- 1¼ teaspoons of sweet paprika
- ½ teaspoon of garlic powder
- ½ teaspoon of onion powder
- ¼ teaspoon of chili powder
- 1/8 teaspoon of black pepper

Cooking Instructions:

1. Preheat your Air fryer to 400°F for about 12 minutes.

2. Lightly spray the Air fryer basket with oil and season pork chops on both sides with ½ teaspoon of kosher salt.

3. In a large shallow bowl, combine the panko, cornflake crumbs, parmesan cheese, ¾ teaspoon of kosher salt, paprika, garlic powder, onion powder, chili powder and black pepper.

4. Then place the beaten egg in another. Dip the pork into the egg, then crumb mixture.

5. Place 3 of the chops into the prepared Air fryer basket and spritz the top with oil.

6. Set your Air fryer to cook for about 12 minutes turning half way, spritzing both sides with oil.

7. Set aside and repeat with the remaining.

8. Serve and enjoy!

Lamb Chop

Serves: 2 people

overall time: 35 mins

Recipe Ingredients:

- 4 lamb chops
- 1½ tbsp. of olive oil
- ½ tbsp. of fresh oregano, finely chopped
- 1 clove of garlic
- Salt
- Ground black pepper

Cooking Instructions:

1. Preheat your Air fryer to 200°C.

2. Lightly coat the clove of garlic with olive oil and place it in your Air Fryer basket.

3. Roast the garlic for about 12 minutes in your Air Fryer. In a medium mixing bowl, mix the herbs with some salt, pepper and olive oil together.

4. Lightly coat the lamb chops with half of the herb oil and allow them to rest for about 3 minutes.

5. Carefully remove the garlic bulb from your Air fryer. Then preheat your Air fryer to 200°C.

6. Place the 4 lamb chops into the Air fryer basket, roast the lamb chops for about 5 minutes till nicely brown.

7. Place them warm in a dish and roast the other lamb chops in the same way. Use your hands to squeeze the garlic cloves over the herb oil.

8. Add some salt and pepper to taste. Give everything a good stir.

9. Serve the lamb chops with garlic sauce.

10. Serve and enjoy!

Chinese Salt & Pepper Pork Chops

Preparation time: 10 minutes

Cooking time: 15 minutes

Overall time: 25 minutes

Serves: 2 people

Recipe Ingredients:

- Pork chops
- 1 egg white
- ½ tsp. of sea salt
- ¼ tsp. of freshly ground black pepper
- ¾ cup of potato starch OR corn starch
- 1 oil mister

Stir fry:

- 2 Jalapeño pepper stems removed, sliced
- 2 scallions (green onions) trimmes, sliced
- 2 tbsp. of canola oil OR peanut
- 1 tsp. of sea salt
- ¼ tsp. of freshly ground black pepper

Cast iron chicken fryer

Cooking Instructions:

1. Start by coating your Air fryer basket with a thin coat of Oil.

2. whisk the egg white, salt and pepper together in a medium mixing bowl until foamy.

3. Slice the pork chops into cutlet pieces, leaving a little on the bones and pat dry.

4. Then add the pork chop pieces to egg white mixture. Coat generously. Marinate for about 20 minutes.

5. In a large bowl, transfer the pork chops and add Potato Starch. Dredge the pork chops through the Potato Starch thoroughly.

6. Shake off pork and place into your prepared Air fryer Basket. Lightly spray pork with Oil.

7. Set your Air fryer to cook at 360°F for about 9 minutes. Shake the basket often and spraying with oil between shakes.

8. Set your Air fryer to cook an additional 6 minutes at 400°F. Slice Jalapeños thin and remove seeds. ¾

9. Chop scallions. Place in bowl and set aside. Heat your skillet until screaming hot.

10. Add in oil, Jalapeño peppers, Scallions, salt and pepper together and stir fry for 1 minute.

11. Add air fried pork pieces to your skillet and toss them with the Jalapeño and Scallions.

12. Stir Fry pork for another minute, ensuring they become coated with the hot oil and vegetables.

13. When the time is up, serve and enjoy!

Turkey Breast with Maple Mustard Glaze

Serves: 5 to 6 people

Recipe Ingredients:

- 2 tsp. of olive oil
- 5 lb. of whole turkey breast
- 1 tsp. of dried thyme
- ½ tsp. of dried sage
- ½ tsp. of smoked paprika
- 1 tsp. of salt
- ½ tsp. of freshly ground black pepper
- ¼ cup of maple syrup
- 2 tbsp. of Dijon mustard
- 1 tbsp. of butter

Cooking Instructions:

1. Preheat your Air fryer to 350°F. Then brush the olive oil all over the turkey breast.

2. In a small mixing bowl, combine the thyme, sage, paprika, salt and pepper and rub the outside of the turkey breast with the spice mixture.

3. After seasoning the turkey breast, transfer them to your Air fryer basket. Set your Air fryer to air-fry at 350°F for about 25 minutes.

4. After the 25 minutes, turn the turkey breast on its side and air-fry for another 12 minutes.

5. After the 12 minutes, turn the turkey breast on the opposite side and air-fry for another 12 minutes.

6. While the turkey is air-frying. In a small sauce pan, combine the maple syrup, mustard and butter.

7. Once the turkey breast is done cooking, return the turkey breast to an upright position and brush the glaze all over the turkey.

8. Air-fry for a final 5 minutes, until the skin is nicely browned and crispy. After the 5 minutes, Let the turkey rest, loosely tented with foil, for at least 5 minutes.

9. Slice and serve immediately.

10. Serve and enjoy!

Pork Chop

Recipe Ingredients:

- 4 pork chops (1 inch thick)
- 1 tbsp. of steak seasoning (We used Montreal Marinade)
- 1/3 cup of olive oil
- ¼ cup of soy sauce

Cooking Instructions:

1. In a large ziplock bag, add all the ingredients and let it marinade for at least 2 hours.

2. Remove from the bag and shake off the excess marinade. Discard the marinade.

3. Set your Air fryer to air fry at 350°F for about 12 minutes. Flip it halfway, after 6 minutes.

4. When the time is up, let it sit in the Air fryer for about 5 minutes. Serve with your favorite side items like corn, broccoli and salad.

5. Serve immediately and enjoy!

Rib Eye Steak

Serves: 3 to 4 people

Recipe Ingredients:

- 2 lb. of rib eye steak
- 1 tbsp. of steak rub
- 1 tbsp. of olive oil

Cooking Instructions:

1. Preheat your Air fryer to 400°F for about 4 minutes. Season the steak on both sides with rub and olive oil.

2. Place the steak in the basket of your Air fryer. Set your Air fryer to 400°F for about 14 minutes.

3. Flip halfway, After 7 minutes. When time is up, remove steak from your Air fryer.

4. Allow it to rest for about 10 minutes before slicing and serving.

5. Serve and enjoy!

Raspberry Balsamic Smoked Pork Chops

Overall time: 30 minutes

Preparation time: 15 minutes

Cooking time: 15 minutes

Serves: 3 to 4 people

Recipe Ingredients:

- 2 large eggs
- ¼ cup 2% milk
- 1 cup of panko (Japanese) bread crumbs
- 1 cup of finely chopped pecans
- 4 smoked bone-in pork chops (7½ oz. each)
- ¼ cup all-purpose flour
- 1/3 cup of balsamic vinegar
- 2 tbsp. of brown sugar
- 2 tbsp. of seedless raspberry jam
- 1 tbsp. of thawed frozen orange juice concentrate

Cooking Instructions:

1. Preheat your Air fryer to 400°F. Spritz the Air fryer basket with cooking spray.

2. Whisk the eggs and milk together in a shallow bowl. In another shallow bowl, toss bread crumbs with pecans.

3. Coat pork chops thoroughly with flour, shake off excess flour and dip in egg mixture.

4. Dip in crumb mixture, patting to help adhere. Work in batches as needed, place chops in single layer in the basket of your Air fryer.

5. Spritz with cooking spray. Set your Air fryer to cook until golden brown, for about 12 to 15 minutes.

6. Turn halfway through cooking. Spritz with additional cooking spray. When the time is up, remove and keep warm.

7. Repeat with remaining chops. Meanwhile, place remaining ingredients in a small saucepan, bring to a boil.

8. Cook and stir until slightly thickened, for about 6 to 8 minutes.

9. Serve with chops and enjoy!

CHAPTER 8: DESSERT & BREAD RECIPES

Air Baked Molten Lava Cakes

Serves: 3 to 4 people

Recipe Ingredients:

- 1.5 tbsp. of self-rising flour
- tbsp. of Baker's sugar, not powdered
- oz. of unsalted butter
- oz. of dark chocolate, pieces or chopped
- 2 eggs

Cooking Instructions:

1. Preheat your Air fryer to 375°F. Grease and flour 4 standard oven safe ramekins.

2. Then Melt the dark chocolate and butter in your microwave safe bowl on level 7 for about 3 minutes. (Stir throughout).

3. When the time is up, remove from microwave and stir until even consistency.

4. Whisk the eggs and sugar together until pale and frothy. Pour melted chocolate mixture into egg mixture.

5. Stir in flour and use a spatula to combine everything evenly. Fill the ramekins about ¾ full with cake mixture.

6. Bake in the preheated Air fryer at 375°F for about 10 minutes. After the 10 minutes, remove from the Air fryer.

7. Allow to cool in ramekin for about 2 minutes. After the 2 minutes, turn ramekins upside down onto serving plate.

8. tap the bottom with a butter knife to loosen edges. Cake should release from ramekin with little effort and center should appear dark/gooey.

9. Enjoy warm with a raspberry drizzle.

10. Serve and enjoy!

Choc Muffins

Preparation time: 15 minutes

Cooking time: 15 minutes

Overall time: 30 minutes

Recipe Ingredients:

- 200 grams of self-raising
- 225 grams of caster sugar
- 25 grams of cocoa powder
- 75 grams of milk chocolate
- 100 grams of butter
- 2 medium eggs
- 5 tablespoons of milk
- Water
- ½ tsp. of vanilla essence

Cooking Instructions:

1. Preheat your Air fryer to 360°F. In a medium mixing bowl, mix the flour, sugar and cocoa together.

2. Add the butter and rub it to produce a breadcrumbs type consistency. In a separate bowl, mix together the milk and two eggs.

3. In a medium bowl, add together the vanilla essence and the egg and mix well. Add a little water if the mixture is too thick.

4. Bash the milk chocolate in a sandwich bag with a rolling pin to form your desired sizes. Place the chocolate to the mixing bowl and mix well.

5. Spoon the mixture into the little bun cases and add it into your Air fryer. Set your Air fryer to cook for about 9 minutes at 360°F.

6. When the time is up, reduce the heat to 320°F and cook for additional 6 minutes more.

7. After the 6 minutes, serve immediately and enjoy!

Flourless Chocolate Almond Cupcake Gluten Free

Preparation time: 10 minutes

Cooking time: 15 to 18 minutes

Overall time: 20 to 22 minutes

Yield: 5 cupcakes

Recipe Ingredients:

- 3 tablespoons of butter (We used smart balance)
- 2 tablespoons of real maple syrup
- ½ cup of almond flour
- 1/8 teaspoon of salt
- 1/3 cup of chocolate chips (We use 60% Ghirardelli)
- 1 egg beaten
- ½ teaspoon of vanilla

Cooking Instructions:

1. Preheat your Air fryer to 320°F. Use silicone cupcake liners.

2. In a stainless-steel bowl, add the chocolate chips, butter and honey and heat over a double boiler for a few seconds, until chocolate starts to melt.

3. When the chocolate begins to melt, remove the bowl and begin stirring until the butter, honey and chocolate are well blended.

4. Allow it to cool for about 7 minutes. Add the remaining ingredients to the cooled melted chocolate.

5. Give everything a good stir with a wooden spoon. Scoop the batter into the prepared cupcake pan.

6. Bake for about 8 to 12 minutes, if toothpick does not come out clean, continue to cook for about 3 to 4 minutes.

7. Top with slivered almonds and unsweetened shredded coconut (optional).

8. Sprinkle with powdered sugar.

9. Serve and enjoy!

Eggless Semolina Cake

Preparation time: 30 minutes

Cooking time: 30 minutes

Overall time: 1 hour

Servings: 5 to 6 people

Recipe Ingredients:

- 1 cup of dried fruit
- 2 cups of hot water
- 1 cup of fine farina or rava
- 1 cup of milk
- 1 cup of sugar
- ¼ cup of ghee, melted butter, or coconut oil
- ¼ cup of sour cream or plain yogurt
- 1 tsp. of ground cardamom
- 1 teaspoon of baking powder
- ½ teaspoon of baking soda

Cooking Directions:

1. Start by soaking the dried fruit in hot water and set dried fruit aside to plump up.

2. Generously grease an 8-inch heat-safe baking pan and set it aside. In a large bowl, whisk together the farina, milk, sugar, ghee, sour cream, and cardamom.

3. Set the mixture aside for about 20 minutes to enable the farina to soften and absorb some of the liquid.

4. Drain the dried fruit and mix it thoroughly with the batter. Add the baking powder and baking soda and give everything a good mix.

5. Pour the cake mix into the greased pan and carefully place the pan into the Air Fryer basket.

6. Set your Air fryer to 330°F to cook for about 25 minutes. Check for doneness at the end of the cooking time, by inserting a toothpick.

7. When the toothpick comes out clean, remove the pan and allow it to rest for about 10 minutes before you unmold the cake.

8. Serve and enjoy.

Chocolate Cake

Preparation time: 10 minutes

Cooking time: 25 minutes

overall time: 35 minutes

Serves: 3 to 4 people

Recipe Ingredients:

- 3 eggs
- ½ cup of sour cream
- 1 cup of flour
- 2/3 cup of sugar
- 1 stick butter room temperature
- 1/3 cup of cocoa powder
- 1 tsp. of baking powder
- ½ tsp. of baking soda
- 2 tsp. of vanilla

Cooking Ingredients:

1. Preheat your Air fryer to 320°F. Mix ingredients on low.

2. Pour into oven attachment and place in your Air fryer basket.

3. Slide into the Air fryer and Set timer to 25 minutes. When the time is up, use toothpick to see if cake is done.

4. If it does not spring back when touched, then cook for an additional 5 minutes.

5. Cool cake on a wire rack. Ice with your favorite chocolate frosting.

6. Serve and enjoy!

Air-Fried Flax Seed French Toast Sticks with Berries

Overall time: 1 hour

Serves: 4

Recipe Ingredients:

- 4 (1½ -oz.) whole-grain bread slices
- 2 large eggs
- ¼ cup 2% reduced-fat milk
- 1 tsp. of vanilla extract
- ½ tsp. of ground cinnamon
- ¼ cup of packed light brown sugar, divided
- 2/3 cup of flax seed meal
- Cooking spray
- 2 cups of sliced fresh strawberries
- 8 tsp. of pure maple syrup, divided
- 1 tsp. of powdered sugar

Cooking Instructions:

1. Start by cutting each slice of bread into 4 long sticks.

2. In a shallow dish, beat the eggs, milk, vanilla, cinnamon, and 1 tbsp. of the brown sugar together.

3. In a second shallow dish, mix the flax seed meal and the remaining 3 tbsp. of brown sugar.

4. Dip bread pieces in egg mixture, slightly soaking them, and allow any excess egg mixture to drip off.

5. Dredge each piece in flax seed mixture, coating on all sides. Coat bread pieces with cooking spray.

6. Place the bread pieces in a single layer in the basket of your Air fryer. leaving room between each piece.

7. Set your Air fryer to cook in batches at 375°F until golden brown and crunchy, for about 10 minutes.

8. Turn the pieces over, after 5 minutes. Place 4 French toast sticks on each plate. Top with ½ cup of strawberries, 2 tsp. of maple syrup, and a sprinkle of powdered sugar.

9. Serve immediately and enjoy!

Baked Apple

Serves: 2 people

Recipe Ingredients:

- 1 medium apple or pear
- 2 tablespoons of chopped walnuts
- 2 tablespoons of raisins
- 1½ teaspoon of light margarine, melted
- ¼ teaspoon of cinnamon
- ¼ teaspoon of nutmeg
- ¼ cup of water

Cooking Instructions:

1. Preheat your Air fryer to 350°F.

2. Start by cutting the apple or pear in half around the middle. Spoon out some of the flesh.

3. Place the apple or pear in your frying pan (which may be provided with the air fryer) or on the bottom of the air fryer (after removing the accessory).

4. Combine margarine, cinnamon, nutmeg, walnuts and raisins in a small mixing bowl.

5. Spoon the mixture into the centers of the apple/pear halves. Then Pour water into the pan.

6. Set your Air fryer to bake for about 20 minutes.

7. When the time is up, serve and enjoy!

Peppermint Lava Cakes

Overall time: 30 minutes

Serve: 3 to 4 people

Recipe Ingredients:

- 2/3 cup of semisweet chocolate chips
- ½ cup of butter, cubed
- 1 cup of confectioners' sugar
- 2 large eggs
- 2 large egg yolks
- 1 tsp. of peppermint extract
- 6 tbsp. of all-purpose flour
- 2 tbsp. of finely crushed peppermint candies (optional)

Cooking Instructions:

1. Preheat your Air fryer to 375°. Melt the chocolate chips and butter in a microwave safe bowl for about 30 seconds, stir until smooth.

2. Whisk in confectioners' sugar, eggs, egg yolks and extract until blended. Fold in flour.

3. Generously grease and flour four, 4-oz. ramekins, pour batter into ramekins.

4. Do not overfill. Place ramekins in the basket of your Air fryer. Set your Air fryer to cook until the edges of cakes are set, for about 10 to 12 minutes.

5. Do not overcook. When the time is up, remove from oven, allow it to sit for about 5 minutes.

6. Carefully run a knife around sides of ramekins several times to loosen cake.

7. Sprinkle with crushed candies. Serve immediately and enjoy!

Apple Dumplings

Preparation time: 25 minutes

Overall time: 35 minutes

Serves: 2

Recipe Ingredients:

- 2 very small apples
- 2 tbsp. of raisins or sultanas
- 1 tbsp. of brown sugar
- 2 sheets of puff pastry
- 2 tbsp. of butter, melted

Cooking Instructions:

1. Preheat the Air fryer to 356°F. Core and peel the apples.

2. In a small mixing bowl, mix the raisins or sultanas and the brown sugar together.

3. Place each apple on 1 of the puff pastry sheets. Fill the core with the raisins or sultanas and sugar mixture.

4. Fold the pastry around the apple so it is fully covered. Place the apple dumplings on a small sheet of foil,

5. Brush the dough with the melted butter. Place in your Air fryer and set your Air fryer to Bake for about 25 minutes.

6. Bake until golden brown and the apples are soft. Turn the apples over once during cooking so that they will cook evenly.

7. When the time is up, allow it to cool for about 10 minutes.

8. Serve with ice cream if desired. Serve and enjoy!

Wasabi Crab Cakes

Overall time: 30 minutes

Preparation time: 20 minutes

Cooking time: 10 minutes

Makes: 2 dozen (½ cup of sauce)

Recipe Ingredients:

- 1 medium sweet red pepper (finely chopped)
- 1 celery rib (finely chopped)
- 3 green onions (finely chopped)
- 2 large egg whites
- 3 tbsp. of reduced-fat mayonnaise
- ¼ tsp. of prepared wasabi
- ¼ tsp. of salt
- 1/3 cup plus ½ cup of dry bread crumbs, divided
- 1½ cups of lump crabmeat, drained
- Cooking spray

Sauce:

- 1 celery rib, chopped
- 1/3 cup of reduced-fat mayonnaise
- 1 green onion, chopped
- 1 tbsp. of sweet pickle relish
- ½ tsp. of prepared wasabi
- ¼ tsp. of celery salt

Cooking Instructions:

1. Preheat your Air fryer to 375°F and spritz the Air fryer basket with cooking spray.

2. Combine the first seven ingredients, add 1/3 cup of bread crumbs and fold in crab gently.

3. In a shallow bowl, place the remaining bread crumbs. Drop heaping tablespoonfuls of crab mixture into crumbs.

4. Gently coat and shape into ¾ -in.-thick patties. Work in batches as needed. Place crab cakes in a single layer in the basket of your Air fryer.

5. Spritz crab cakes with cooking spray and cook until golden brown for about 8 to 12 minutes.

6. turn halfway through cooking, spritzing with additional cooking spray. Remove and keep warm.

7. Repeat with remaining crab cakes. Place sauce ingredients in a food processor, pulse two to three times to blend.

8. Serve crab cakes immediately with dipping sauce.

9. Serve and enjoy!

5 Ingredient Chocolate Mug Cake

Preparation time: 2 mins

Cooking time: 10 minutes

Total time: 12 minutes

Serves: 1

Recipe Ingredients:

- ¼ cup of self-rising flour
- 5 tbsp. of caster sugar
- 1 tablespoon of cocoa powder
- 3 tablespoons of whole milk
- 3 teaspoons of coconut oil

Cooking Instructions:

1. Start by mixing all the ingredients together in the mug. Mix well to combine.

2. Place the mug in your Air fryer. Set your Air fryer to cook for about 10 minutes at 200°C.

3. Rinse and repeat for the other mugs until everyone has had their chocolate hit!

4. Serve immediately and enjoy!

Cinnamon Bananas

Preparation time: 15 minutes

Cooking time: 7 minutes

Overall time: 22 minutes

Recipe Ingredients:

- 3 tbsp. of coconut oil
- 8 ripe bananas
- 2 eggs
- ½ cup of corn flour
- 3 tbsp. of cinnamon sugar
- 1 cup of panko bread crumb

Cooking Instructions:

1. Preheat your Air fryer to 280°F. Add coconut oil in a pan on medium heat on the stove and add the bread crumbs.

2. Give everything a good stir for about 3 to 4 minutes, or until it turns a light golden color.

3. In a medium mixing bowl, beat the eggs and add the corn flour. Peel and halve the bananas.

4. Roll each of the banana half in corn flour, eggs, and bread crumbs and make sure that the mixtures covers the bread crumbs.

5. Place the coated banana halves side by side in your Air fryer basket in a single layer. You can also cook in batches and dust it with the cinnamon sugar.

6. Set your Air fryer to cook for about 7 minutes at 280°F. when the time is up, carefully remove cinnamon bananas from your Air fryer basket.

7. Place on serving plate. Serve and enjoy!

CHAPTER 9: VEGEARIAN MAIN DISHES

Air Fried Spicy Cauliflower Stir-Fry

Preparation time: 5 minutes

Cooking time: 25 minutes

Overall time: 30 minutes

Serves: 3 to 4 people

Recipe Ingredients:

- 1 head cauliflower cut into florets
- ¾ cup of onion white, thinly sliced
- 5 cloves of garlic, finely sliced
- 1½ tbsp. of tamari or gluten free tamari
- 1 tbsp. of rice vinegar
- ½ tsp. of coconut sugar
- 1 tbsp. of Sriracha or other favourite hot sauce
- 2 scallions for garnish

Cooking Instructions:

1. Start by Placing cauliflower in your Air fryer. If your air fryer is one that has holes in the bottom, you'll need to use an air fryer insert.

2. Set your Air fryer to 350°F and cook cauliflower for about 10 minutes. When the time is up, open your Air fryer.

3. Grab the pot by the handle, remove and shake. Slide back in the compartment.

4. Add in the sliced onion, give everything a good stir and cook for more 10 minutes.

5. Add in garlic, stir and cook more 5 minutes. In a small mixing bowl, mix soy sauce, rice vinegar, coconut sugar, Sriracha, salt & pepper together.

6. Add the mixture to cauliflower and give everything a good stir. Cook for 5 more minutes.

7. The insert keeps all of the juices inside. To serve sprinkle sliced scallions over the top for garnish.

8. Serve and enjoy!

Vegan Bacon Wrapped Mini Breakfast Burritos

Serve: 2

Recipe Ingredients:

- 2 tbsp. of cashew butter
- 2 to 3 tbsp. of tamari
- 1 to 2 tbsp. of liquid smoke
- 1 to 2 tbsp. of water
- 4 pieces rice paper
- Vegan egg scramble or Tofu scramble

veggie add ins:

- ⅓ cup of roasted sweet potato cubes
- 8 strips of roasted red pepper
- 1 small tree broccoli, sautéed
- 6 to 8 stalks fresh asparagus
- handful spinach, kale, other greens

Cooking Instructions:

1. Preheat your oven to 350°F. Line baking sheet with parchment.

2. Whisk the cashew butter, tamari, liquid smoke, and water together in a small mixing bowl. Set aside.

3. Prepare all fillings to assemble rolls. have a large plate/surface ready to fill/roll wrapper.

4. Hold one rice paper under water faucet running cool water, getting both sides of wrapper wet, for few seconds.

5. Then remove the rice paper from water. While still firm, place on plate to fill, rice paper will soften as it sits.

6. Fill by placing the ingredients just off from the middle, leaving sides of rice paper free.

7. Fold the two sides in like a burrito, roll from ingredient side to other side, and seal.

8. Start Dipping each roll into cashew - liquid smoke mixture, coat them thoroughly and arrange rolls on parchmented baking sheet.

9. Place them in your Air fryer and set your Air Fryer to cook these at 350°F for about 8 to 10 minutes, or until crisp. Serve warm and enjoy!

Avocado Egg Rolls with Sweet Chili Sauce

Preparation time: 20 minutes

Cooking time: 25 minutes

Serves: 4 to 5 people

Recipe Ingredients:

- 10 egg roll wrappers
- 3 avocados, peeled and pitted
- 1 roma tomato diced
- ½ tsp. of salt
- ¼ tsp. of pepper
- Canola oil for frying

For the sweet chili sauce:

- 4 tbsp. of sriracha
- 2 tbsp. of white sugar
- 1 tbsp. of rice vinegar
- 1 tbsp. of sesame oil

Cooking Instructions:

1. In a medium mixing bowl, add avocados, tomato, salt, and pepper.

2. Mash the avocados to a chunky consistency and give everything a good stir to combine the ingredients. (This will become the egg roll filling).

3. Lay out the egg roll wrappers and a small bowl of water. Distribute the egg roll filling among the wrappers.

4. Scoop them onto the bottom third of each wrapper. Taking one wrapper at a time.

5. Then use a finger to brush water along its four edges, fold up a corner over the filling, then roll up the sides.

6. Dab the last fold with more water to seal. Repeat the process for all other wrappers.

7. In a large pot, add in canola oil until the oil is about 2 inches deep. Turn the burner to medium heat.

8. When the oil temperature reaches 350°F, add the egg rolls in batches. Allow it to cook until golden brown, for about 3 minutes.

9. When the time in up, Transfer to a paper towel to drain and slice each egg roll diagonally.

10. In a small mixing bowl, combine sauce ingredients and mix together.

11. Serve with sliced avocado egg rolls.

12. Serve and enjoy!

Taco Crunch Wrap

Recipe Ingredients:

- 1 regular size of gluten free tortilla
- 2 tbsp. of grated cheese
- 2 small corn of tortillas
- 2 tbsp. of refried pinto beans
- 2 tbsp. of guacamole
- Iceberg lettuce

Cooking Instructions:

1. First preheat your Air Fryer to 350°F.

2. Assemble each crunch wrap by stacking in the following order, large regular tortilla, cheese, small corn tortilla, beans, guacamole, lettuce, and the second small corn tortilla.

3. Carefully fold and turn the wrap with your hands more cheese to seal. Set your Air fryer to cook the taco crunch wrap for about 6 minutes at 350°F.

4. Bake it at 325°F for about 5 to 8 minutes, or until it has warmed through and slightly crispy.

5. After baking, serve immediately with dairy free sour cream and guacamole for dipping.

6. Make use of the mashed avocado, lemon juice and sea salt to prepare the guacamole.

7. Serve and enjoy!

Bow Tie Pasta Chips

Recipe Ingredients:

- 2 cups f dry whole wheat bow tie pasta (use brown rice pasta)
- 1 tbsp. of olive oil
- 1 tbsp. of nutritional yeast
- 1½ tsp. of Italian seasoning blend
- ½ tsp. of salt

Cooking Instructions:

1. Start by Cooking the pasta for ½ the time called for on the package.

2. Toss the drained pasta with the olive oil, nutritional yeast, Italian seasoning, and salt.

3. Place about half of the mixture in the Air fryer basket. Cook in two batch if your Air fryer basket is small.

4. Set your Air fryer to cook at 390°F for about 5 minutes. After the 5 minutes.

5. Shake the basket and cook for 3 to 5 minutes more or until crunchy.

6. When the time is up, serve and enjoy!

Toasted Coconut French Toast

Preparation time: 6 minutes

Cooking time: 4 minutes

Overall time: 10 minutes

Serves: 1

Recipe Ingredients:

- 2 slices of gluten-free bread (use your favorite)
- ½ cup of lite culinary coconut milk
- 1 teaspoon of baking powder
- ½ cup of unsweetened shredded coconut

Cooking Instructions:

1. Start by mixing the coconut milk and baking powder together in a wild rimmed bowl.

2. Spread the shredded coconut out on a plate. Take each slice of bread and first soak in the coconut milk mixture.

3. Few seconds before transferring to the shredded coconut plate and fully coating the slice in the coconut milk mixture.

4. In your Air fryer, space both the coated slices of bread, close it. Set your Air fryer to 350°F and cook for about 4 minutes.

5. When the time is up, remove and top with maple syrup or your favorite French toast toppings.

6. Serve immediately and enjoy!

Fried Ravioli

Preparation time: 5 minutes

Cooking time: 5 minutes

Overall time: 10 minutes

Serves: 5 to 6 people

Recipe Ingredients:

- 1(14-oz.) jar marinara sauce
- 1(9-oz.) box cheese ravioli, store-bought or meat ravioli
- 1 tsp. of olive oil
- 2 cups of Italian-style bread crumbs
- 1 cup of buttermilk
- ¼ cup of Parmesan cheese

Cooking Directions:

1. Start by dipping ravioli in buttermilk and add olive oil to breadcrumbs.

2. Press the ravioli into it. Put breaded ravioli into the heated Air fryer on baking paper.

3. Set your Air fryer to cook at 200°F for about 5 minutes.

4. Serve warm with marinara sauce for dipping.

5. Serve immediately and enjoy!

Vegan Cheesy Potato Wedges

Preparation time: 15 minutes

Cooking time: 16 minutes

Overall time: 31 minutes

Serves: 3 to 4 people

Recipe Ingredients:

For the Potatoes:

- 1 pound of fingerling potatoes
- 1 teaspoon of extra virgin olive oil
- 1 teaspoon of kosher salt
- 1 teaspoon of ground black pepper
- ½ teaspoon of garlic powder

For the Cheese Sauce:

- ½ cup of raw cashews
- ½ teaspoon of ground turmeric
- ½ teaspoon of paprika
- 2 tablespoons of nutritional yeast
- 1 teaspoon of fresh lemon juice
- 2 tbsp. to ¼ cup of water

Cooking Instructions:

1. Preheat your Air fryer to 400°F for about 3 minutes.

2. Wash the potatoes in clean water. Cut the potatoes in half lengthwise, transfer the potatoes to a large bowl.

3. Add the in oil, salt, pepper, and garlic powder to the potatoes. Toss to coat and transfer them to your Air fryer.

4. Set your Air fryer to cook for about 16 minutes. Shake halfway through the cooking time.

5. In a high-speed blender, combine the cashews, turmeric, paprika, nutritional yeast, and lemon juice together.

6. Blend on low, slowly increasing the speed and adding water as needed. Do not add too much water.

7. Transfer the cooked potatoes to your Air fryer safe pan or a piece of parchment paper.

8. Drizzle the cheese sauce over the potato wedges and place the pan in your Air fryer.

9. Set your Air fryer to cook for 2 more minutes at 400°F.

10. When the time is up, serve and enjoy!

Sticky Mushroom Rice

Preparation time: 5 minutes

Cooking time: 20 minutes

Overall time: 25 minutes

Serves: 5 to 6 people

Recipe Ingredients:

- 16 oz. jasmine rice uncooked
- ½ cup of soy sauce (you can use gluten free tamari)
- 4 tbsp. of maple syrup
- 4 cloves of garlic, finely chopped
- 2 tsp. of Chinese 5 spice
- ½ tsp. of ground ginger
- 4 tbsp. of white wine (you can use rice vinegar)
- 16 oz. cremini mushrooms wiped clean (you can cut any huge mushrooms in half)
- ½ cup of peas frozen

Cooking Instructions:

1. Start your rice now so that it will be done and hot at the same time as the sauce.

2. Mix the first 6 ingredients together and set aside. Place the mushrooms in your Air fryer.

3. Set your Air fryer to 350°F and cook for about 10 minutes. When the time is up.

4. Open your air fryer, pull out the pot and shake. Pour the liquid mixture and peas over the top of the mushrooms.

5. Give everything a good stir and cook for more 5 minutes. Pour the mushroom/pea sauce over the pot of rice and stir.

6. Serve immediately and enjoy!

Cauliflower Chickpea Tacos

Preparation time: 10 minutes

Cooking time: 20 minutes

Total time: 30 minutes

Serves: 3 to 4 people

Recipe Ingredients:

- 4 cups of cauliflower florets, cut into bite-sized pieces
- 19 ounces can of chickpeas drained and rinsed
- 2 tbsp. of olive oil
- 2 tbsp. of taco seasoning

To serve:

- 8 small tortillas
- 2 avocados, sliced
- 4 cups of cabbage shredded
- Coconut yogurt to drizzle

Cooking Instructions:

1. Preheat your Air fryer to 390°F/ 200°C.

2. Toss the cauliflower and chickpeas in a large bowl. Toss with the olive oil and taco seasoning.

3. Place them into the basket of your Air fryer. Set your Air fryer to cook for about 20 minutes, shake the basket occasionally until cooked through.

4. Cauliflower will be golden but not burnt. Serve in tacos with avocado slices, cabbage and coconut yogurt.

5. Serve immediately and enjoy!

Thai Veggie Bites

Preparation time: 5 minutes

Cooking time: 20 minutes

Overall time: 25 minutes

Recipe Ingredients:

- 1 large broccoli
- 1 large cauliflower
- 6 large carrots
- Handful garden peas
- ½ cauliflower made into cauliflower rice
- 1 large onion, peeled and diced
- 1 small courgette
- 2 leeks cleaned and thinly sliced
- 1 can of coconut milk
- 50g plain flour
- 1 cm cube of ginger, peeled and grated
- 1 tablespoon of garlic puree
- 1 tablespoon of olive oil
- 1 tablespoon of Thai green curry paste
- 1 tablespoon of coriander
- 1 tablespoon of mixed spice
- 1 teaspoon of cumin
- Salt & pepper to taste

Cooking Instructions:

1. In a wok, cook your onion, garlic, ginger and olive oil until the onion has a good bit of color on it.

2. During the Onion cooking process. In a steamer, cook your vegetables (apart from the courgette and leek) for about 20 minutes.

3. Then add in the courgette, the leek and the curry paste to your wok. Cook on a medium heat for about 5 minutes more.

4. Add the coconut milk and the remaining seasoning, mix together and then add the cauliflower rice.

5. Mix again and allow simmering for about 10 minutes. Once it has simmered for about 10 minutes.

6. The sauce has reduced by half, add the steamed vegetables. Mix well and you will now have a lovely base for your veggie bites.

7. Place in the fridge for an hour to cool. After one hour, make into bite sizes. Place it in your Air fryer.

8. Set your Air fryer to cook for about 10 minutes at 180°C.

9. When the time is up, serve with a cooling dip and enjoy!

Garlic and Herb Air-Fryer Roasted Chickpeas

Preparation time: 5 minutes

Cooking time: 20 minutes

Overall time: 25 minutes

Serves: 3 to 4 people

Recipe Ingredients:

- 2 cans of chickpeas
- 1 tablespoon of olive oil
- 1 tablespoon of nutritional yeast
- 2 teaspoon of garlic powder
- 1 tablespoon of mixed herbs (rosemary, thyme, and oregano work well)
- Sea salt & black pepper to taste

Cooking Instructions:

1. Drain and rinse the chickpeas. Add the chickpeas to a medium-sized mixing bowl.

2. Add in the olive oil and seasonings. Use a spatula to give everything a good stir to combine well.

3. Ensure that all the chickpeas are well coated. Then divide the chickpeas and cook in two batches in the air-fryer.

4. Set your Air fryer to cook at 200°C for about 15 to 20 minutes. stir once at the 10-minute mark.

5. You may hear some popping while they're cooking which is totally normal.

6. They're done once they're golden brown and crispy. Serve while warm and store in an air-tight jar once cooled to preserve crispiness.

7. Serve and enjoy!

CHAPTER 10: KETOGENIC DIET RECIPES

Crispy Keto Parmesan Crusted Pork Chops

Preparation time: 5 minutes

Cooking time: 15 minutes

Overall time: 20 minutes

Serves: 3 to 4 people

Recipe Ingredients:

- 4 to 6 thick center cut boneless pork chops
- ½ tsp. of salt
- ¼ teaspoon of pepper
- 1 teaspoon of smoked paprika
- ½ teaspoon of onion powder
- ¼ teaspoon of chili powder
- 2 large eggs, beaten
- 1 cup of pork rind crumbs
- 3 tbsp. of grated parmesan cheese

Cooking Instructions:

1. Preheat your Air fryer to 400°F for about 10 minutes. Then generously season both sides of each pork chop with salt and pepper.

2. Using a food processor, blend the pork rinds into crumbs. In a medium bowl, combine together the pork rind crumbs and seasonings.

3. In a separate egg, place the beaten egg. Dip each of the pork chop into the egg, then the crumb mixture secondly.

4. Place each of the pork chop in your Air fryer basket. Set your Air fryer to cook the pork chops in batches at 400°F for about 12 to 15 minutes.

5. Serve and enjoy.

Beef Keema Meatloaf

Preparation time: 10 minutes

Cooking time: 18 minutes

Overall time: 28 minutes

Serves: 3 to 4 people

Recipe Ingredients:

- 1 pound of ground beef
- 2 eggs
- 1 cup of onion, diced
- ¼ cup of cilantro, chopped
- 1 tablespoon of minced ginger
- 1 tbsp. garlic, minced
- 2 teaspoons of garam masala
- 1 tsp. of salt
- 1 teaspoon of turmeric
- 1 teaspoon of cayenne
- ½ teaspoon of ground cinnamon
- 1/8 teaspoon of ground cardamom

Cooking Directions:

1. In a medium bowl, combine together all the ingredients and mix thoroughly until it has well mixed.

2. Place the seasoned meat into a heat-safe, 8-inch round pan and set your Air fryer to 360°F for about 15 minutes.

3. After the 15 minutes, measure it with a meat thermometer and ensure that the meatloaf has reached an internal temperature of 160°F.

4. Remove the meatloaf from the pan and drain the excess fat and liquid. Slice it into 4 pieces and top with your Keema loaf.

5. Serve and enjoy!

Low Carb Fried Chicken

Preparation time: 10 minutes

Cooking time: 50 minutes

Soak time: 2 hours

Overall time: 1 hour

Serves: 8 to 10 people

Recipe Ingredients:

- 5 lb. of chicken, about 10 pieces
- 1 cup of almond milk
- 1 tbsp. of white vinegar
- 2 cups of crushed pork rinds
- ½ tsp. of salt
- ½ tsp. of thyme
- ½ tsp. of basil
- 1/3 tsp. of oregano
- 1 tsp. of celery salt
- 1 tsp. of black pepper
- 1 tsp. of dried mustard
- 4 tsp. of paprika
- 2 tsp. of garlic salt
- 1 tsp. of ground ginger
- 3 tsp. of white pepper
- 1 tbsp. of coconut oil

Cooking Instructions:

1. Start by Placing chicken in a large bowl. Mix almond milk and vinegar together, pour the mixture over chicken.

2. Allow the chicken to soak in the liquid for about 2 hours in the refrigerator. In wide shallow bowl.

3. Combine the pork rinds, salt, thyme, basil, oregano, celery salt, black pepper, dried mustard, paprika, garlic salt, ground ginger, and white pepper together.

4. Coat the chicken by dipping each piece of chicken in dry pork rind mixture. Spread 1 tbsp. of coconut oil in the bottom of your Air fryer basket.

5. Arrange the chicken in single layer on the Air fryer basket. Set your Air fryer to Air fry at 360°F for about 10 minutes.

6. After the 10 minutes, rotate the chicken and air fry for another 10 minutes. Test chicken temperature to reach 165°F.

7. Continue cooking if needed, when the time is up.

8. Serve and enjoy!

Keto Chinese-Style Spareribs

Preparation time: 40 minutes

Cooking time: 10 minutes

Overall time: 50 minutes

Serves: 3 to 4 people

Recipe Ingredients:

- 1 tbsp. of sesame oil
- 1 tsp. of minced garlic
- 1 tsp. of minced ginger
- 1 tbsp. of fermented black bean paste
- 1 tbsp. of Shaoxing wine
- 1 tablespoon of dark soy sauce
- 1 tbsp. of agave nectar or honey
- 1.5 lb. of spareribs cut into small pieces

Cooking Instructions:

1. In a medium bowl, stir together all ingredients for the marinade. Add the spare ribs and mix everything to combine.

2. Let the ribs to marinade for about 30 minutes or up to 24 hours in the refrigerator.

3. Remove the ribs from the marinade, place the ribs in the basket of your Air fryer.

4. Set your Air fryer at 375°F for about 8 minutes. Check to ensure the ribs have an internal temperature of 165°F with a meat thermometer.

5. When the time is up, serve and enjoy!

Low-Carb Cauliflower Buffalo Wings

Preparation time: 5 minutes

Cooking time: 15 minutes

Overall time: 20 minutes

Serves: 3 to 4 people

Recipe Ingredients:

- 1 head cauliflower, cut into small bites
- Cooking oil spray
- ½ cup of buffalo sauce
- 1 tbsp. of butter melted
- Salt and pepper to taste

Cooking Instructions:

1. Start by spraying the Air fryer basket with cooking oil. In a small mixing bowl, Add the melted butter, buffalo sauce, and salt and pepper to taste.

2. Give everything a good stir to combine. Add the cauliflower bites to your Air fryer.

3. Spray the cauliflower with cooking oil. Set your Air fryer to cook for about 7 minutes at 400°.

4. When the time is up, open the Air fryer and place the cauliflower in a large mixing bowl.

5. Drizzle the butter and buffalo mixture throughout. Stir everything together. Add the cauliflower back to your Air fryer.

6. Set your Air fryer to cook for an additional 7 to 8 minutes at 400°F until the cauliflower wings are crisp.

7. Every air fryer brand is different. Ensure to use your personal judgment to assist with optimal cook time.

8. When the time is up, remove the cauliflower from your Air fryer.

9. Serve with homemade keto ranch dressing.

10. Serve and enjoy!

Bacon and Cream Cheese Stuffed Jalapeno Poppers

Preparation time: 10 minutes

Cooking time: 5 minutes

Overall time: 15 minutes

Serves: 4 to 5 people

Recipe Ingredients:

- 10 fresh jalapenos
- 6 ounces of cream cheese (We used reduced-fat)
- ¼ cup of shredded cheddar cheese
- 2 slices of bacon cooked and crumbled
- Cooking oil spray

Cooking Instruction:

1. Start by slicing the jalapenos in half, vertically, to create 2 halves per jalapeno.

2. In a small bowl, place the cream cheese. Microwave for about 15 seconds to soften.

3. After the 15 seconds, remove the seeds and the inside of the jalapeno. Save some of the seeds if you prefer spicy poppers.

4. In a medium bowl, combine the cream cheese, crumbled bacon, and shredded cheese together. Mix together to combine.

5. For extra spicy poppers, add some of the seeds to the cream cheese mixture, and mix well.

6. Stuff each of the jalapenos with the cream cheese mixture. Load the poppers into your Air fryer.

7. Spray the poppers with cooking oil. Set your Air fryer to cook the poppers at 370°F for about 5 minutes.

8. When the time is up, remove from the Air fryer and cool before serving.

9. Serve immediately and enjoy!

CHAPTER 11: EGG RECIPES

Air-Baked Eggs

Overall time: 30 minutes

Serves: 4

Recipe Ingredients:

- 7 oz. (200g) leg ham, sliced
- 1 pound (500g) baby spinach
- 4 large eggs, refrigerated
- 4 tbsp. of full cream milk
- 1 tbsp. of olive oil
- Unsalted butter
- Salt and pepper

Cooking Instructions:

1. Preheat your Air fryer to 350°F (180°C). Use the butter to butter up the 4 ramekins.

2. On the stove, heat up the olive oil and cook the baby spinach until it is wilted. After cooking baby spinach, drain off any excess water or other liquids.

3. Divide out the cooked spinach equally over the four ramekins. Divide the ham equally over the four ramekins.

4. Crack an egg into each ramekin and add a tbsp. of milk. Sprinkle to taste with salt and pepper.

5. Bake for 15 to 20 minutes or (until the egg white sets).

6. When the time is up, serve and enjoy!

Baked Eggs in Bread Bowls

Overall time: 25 to 30 minutes

Serves: 4

Recipe Ingredients:

- 4 crusty dinner rolls (or as many as you choose)
- 4 large eggs
- 4 tbsp. of mixed herbs, chopped (parsley, chives, tarragon)
- 4 tbsp. of heavy cream
- Salt and pepper to taste
- Parmesan cheese, grated

Cooking Instructions:

1. Slice off top of each dinner roll, carefully remove some bread until there is a hole large enough to accommodate an egg.

2. Arrange the rolls on a baking sheet. Reserve tops. Then crack an egg into each roll. Top each egg with some herbs and a bit of cream.

3. Season with salt and pepper. Sprinkle with Parmesan. Bake at a 350°F (180°C) for about 20 to 25 minutes.

4. Bake until eggs are set and bread is toasted. After eggs have cooked for about 20 minutes.

5. Place bread tops on baking sheet, bake until golden brown. When the time is up, allow it to sit for about 5 minutes.

6. Place tops on rolls and serve warm.

7. Serve and enjoy!

Breakfast Souffle

Overall time: 8 to 10 minutes

Serves: 4

Recipe Ingredients:

- 4 eggs
- 4 tbsp. of light cream
- Red chilli pepper
- Parsley

Cooking Instructions:

1. Finely chop the parsley and chilli. In a medium mixing bowl, add in the eggs and stir in the cream, parsley and pepper

2. Fill the dishes up to halfway with the egg mixture and place them in your Air fryer.

3. Bake the soufflés at 392°F (200°C) for about 8 minutes. If you want to serve the soufflés baveux (soft).

4. Then 5 minutes cooking is enough. When the time is up.

5. Serve immediately and enjoy!

Easy Breakfast Sandwich

Serves: 1

Recipe Ingredients:

- 1 free range egg
- 1 English bacon or 2 streaky bacons
- 1 English muffin
- A pinch of pepper and salt

Cooking Instructions:

1. Start by cracking the egg into an ovenproof soufflé cup. Then place the egg, bacon and muffin into your Air-fryer.

2. Set your Air fryer to air-fryer to 392°F (200°C) for about 6 minutes.

3. When the time is up, assemble the sandwich.

4. Serve and enjoy!

Easy Full English

Overall time: 15 to 20 minutes

Serves: 3 to 4 people

Recipe Ingredients:

- 8 chestnut mushrooms
- 8 tomatoes, halved
- 1 clove of garlic, crushed
- 4 rashers of smoked back bacon
- 4 chipolatas
- 7 ounces of (200g) baby leaf spinach
- 4 large eggs

Cooking Instructions:

1. Start by heating your Air fryer to 392°F (200°C). Put the mushrooms, tomatoes and garlic in a round tin.

2. Season the mixture and spray with oil. Place the tin, bacon and chipolatas in your Air fryer cooking basket.

3. Set your Air fryer to cook for about 10 minutes. Meanwhile wilt the spinach in a microwave or by pouring boiling water through it in a sieve. Drain well.

4. Add the spinach to the tin and crack in the eggs. Reduce temperature to 160°C. Set your Air fryer to cook for a further few minutes until the eggs are cooked.

5. When the time is up, serve and enjoy!

Easy Egg Cups

Preparation time: 10 minutes

Cooking time: 10 minutes

Overall time: 20 minutes

Recipe Ingredients

- 6 tbsp. of sausage, cooked & crumbled (divided)
- 6 tbsp. of frozen chopped spinach (divided)
- 6 tsp. of shredded Co-Jack cheese (divided)
- ¼ cup of egg beaters® 99% egg substitute (divided)

Cooking Instructions:

1. Cook your sausage crumbles and keep aside.

2. Grab your muffin cups and layer 1 tablespoon of each sausage crumbles, spinach and 1 teaspoon of cheese into the cups.

3. Pour the egg mixture over the top. Place the muffin cups in your Air fryer basket.

4. Bake at 330°F for about 10 minutes. After the 10 minutes, allow egg cups to cool slightly before eating.

5. Serve warm and enjoy!

Scrambled Eggs

Preparation time: 5 minutes

Cooking time: 9 minutes

Overall time: 10 minutes

Serves: 2

Recipe Ingredients:

- Air fryer baking pan
- 2 slices of wholemeal bread
- 4 large eggs
- Salt & pepper

Cooking Instructions:

1. Warm up the bread at 200°C/400°F for about 3 minutes so that it is harder like toast.

2. Crack the eggs into the Air fryer and give them a quick stir. Add to them the seasoning.

3. Place the baking pan inside your Air fryer. Set your Air fryer to cook for about 2 minutes at 180°C/360°F

4. Give everything a good stir and cook for another 4 minutes at the same temperature.

5. Pour the scrambled eggs over the wholemeal toast.

6. Serve and enjoy!

Whole 30 Bacon & Eggs

Preparation time: 5 minutes

Cooking time: 13 minutes

Overall time: 14 minutes

Serves: 3 to 4 people

Recipe Ingredients:

- 4 ramekins
- 8 back bacon
- 4 large eggs
- Fresh chives (optional)
- Salt & pepper

Cooking Instructions:

1. Get the ramekins out, add the bacon around the sides and bottom of it.

2. So that it overlaps in the same way as when you're making a pastry over an apple pie. Crack an egg into the Centre of each ramekin.

3. Set your Air fryer to cook at 180°C for about 13 minutes. After the 13 minutes.

4. Season with salt and pepper and fresh chives.

5. Serve and enjoy!

Scotch Eggs

serves: 4

Recipe Ingredients:

- 6 eggs, separated
- 1 pound of ground pork sausage
- 1 teaspoon of nutmeg
- ½ teaspoon of dried thyme
- ½ cup of flour
- ½ cup of breadcrumbs

Cooking Instructions:

1. In a small sauce pan filled with water, place the 4 eggs and bring to a boil.

2. When the water begins to boil, set timer for about 4 minutes. When the time is up, remove the pot from heat immediately.

3. Run cold water into the saucepot until eggs are cool to the touch. Peel boiled eggs and keep aside.

4. Add the ground pork sausage, nutmeg, and thyme in a medium mixing bowl. Mix them together to combine.

5. Then divide the mixture into 4 equal sections. Grab one section, pat it out to a flat patty.

6. Place egg in the center, and wrap pork around egg. Repeat the process with the remaining eggs. Preheat your Air fryer to 390°F.

7. While the air fryer is preheating, place the ½ cup of flour into a bowl. Whisk the remaining two eggs into a second bowl.

8. Place the ½ cup of breadcrumbs into a third bowl and roll each pork rolled egg in the flour, then egg, and finally the breadcrumbs.

9. Place the scotch eggs into the tray, once your Air fryer has finished preheating. Set the timer for about 13 minutes.

10. When the time is up, serve and enjoy!

Acknowledgement

In preparing the "Air Fryer Cookbook for Beginners", I sincerely wish to acknowledge my indebtedness to my husband for his support and the wholehearted cooperation and vast experience of my two colleagues - Mrs. Catherine Long, and Mrs. Alexander Bedria.

Alexandra Bryne

Printed in Great Britain
by Amazon